Thrive After 60

How to live your **BEST** life in retirement
AND have financial freedom

A Self-Help Guide for Seniors

Peter Allen Dickinson

5D EARTH
BOOKS

Thrive After 60

Cover design by Peter Allen Dickinson
Book design by Peter Allen Dickinson

Published by **5D Earth Books**

ISBN: 978-1-0684658-0-2

First Edition: 2025
Printed in United Kingdom

This is a work of nonfiction.

For permissions, inquiries, or additional information, contact:
peter@padickinson.co.uk

Acknowledgements

As I have become more 'mature', I have become to realise the important part my parents and siblings played in my life. Without my troubled childhood, I would not be the person I am today. We lived in a steel producing town and I think I myself went through some process of 'forging' in my youth and that shaped my view of the world.

And so, I would like to thank my parents, my three brothers and my two sisters. The five of us that remain have all passed the retirement threshold, which is something of a testament to our endurance, given our disturbed formative years.

We didn't have the best of upbringings but I like to think that we children looked after each other and went on to lead productive lives.

I also need to acknowledge the part my wife Renee has played in my 'growth'. Without her support and understanding I would not have learned the lessons that have shaped my thinking in this book.

Contents

Introduction

A toast to new beginnings: Redefining life after 60

Take a look at a young child under two years old. I mean really watch them. They stare out at the world with wide, curious eyes. They have no doubts about themselves and no limit to their imagination. And they seem to want to laugh at just about anything. Imagine channelling that same youthful spirit into your next stage – life after sixty! That's the feeling I would like to invoke in you. The "Lust for Life" that Iggy Pop sings about.

Turning sixty today is nothing like it was for our grandparents. Forget images of rocking chairs and quiet evenings by the fireplace (though those can be lovely too, on occasion!). You and I should see this as a stage filled with adventure, purpose, and a renewed sense of self.

Society bombards us with stereotypes of frail, out-of-touch seniors, painting a bleak picture of decline and limitations.

This is where I aim to shine a light on those myths and give you the power to achieve <u>your</u> potential.

I am writing this to help you, the person nearing retirement or already living in retirement. To help you realise that you can live the life you want. To help you embrace later life with a positive mindset that keeps you healthy, of sound mind and positive about life. I want you to find the joy you deserve.

My wish is that you benefit from my many decades of learning. And my advice would be to never stop 'growing'. I feel that when we stop 'growing' we are starting to fade and die. I would like to help you enjoy a fulfilling journey from here until we meet our maker.

Farewell to stereotypes

Let's be honest, the whole "life begins at sixty" thing can feel a bit patronising. It implies there's nothing meaningful beforehand, which is simply untrue. Every stage of life holds unique joys and challenges. But the truth is, thanks to amazing advances in medicine, technology, and our collective understanding of ageing, people are living longer, healthier lives than ever before.

Your sixtieth birthday isn't a finish line – it's a springboard! Think of it as a chance to leap into a new phase of exploration, growth, and contribution to the world.

My story

Born in 1953, I was the third of six children living on a council estate, in poverty, with an alcoholic father. By 14 years of age, I discovered alcohol, as a 16 year-old I discovered drugs and by 18 years old, I was in prison. I went completely 'off the rails' and could not see any role for me in 'normal' society. At school aged 14, I went from being an A grade pupil to a 'drop out'. There seemed to be no reason to study because all I saw in front of me was hopelessness. I took to truancy and neither the school nor my parents seemed to care. Consequently, I left school at 16 with one GCE certificate in Woodwork.

There was no role model for me to look up to. There seemed to be no hope of raising myself out of poverty so I was searching for 'escape' from it all. Hence the drugs and alcohol. I felt that being 'numb' to it all was the answer and I searched for ways to stay 'tuned out'.

What changed? Well, I thought I needed to model myself on someone I respected, not my father. My lifesaver was my eldest sister's boyfriend!

He was slightly more mature than my sister and was working as an electrician. Then he joined the Merchant Navy and travelled the world as the ship's "Mr Fixer". When they married, my sister joined him on the ship. That was a life I could relate to. It had adventure and fun but – most of all – he was wanted. There was a position for him, even made for him – he had found his place. That was for me! I wanted to be wanted.

My career

Following in the footsteps of my brother-in-love, I became an apprentice electrician. Then that dream was crushed when I was made redundant after my first year. So, I moved into repairing electronic equipment, which ended up being mostly TV repair.

I struggled on with that for about four years and then I read something about these things called computers. So, I started applying for jobs as a computer engineer (the guy you call when it breaks). I was successful in joining International Computers Limited (ICL) in 1976. I was a young man and felt I had landed somewhere where I belonged, so I gave everything of myself to fixing computers.

We didn't have personal computers in those days and just one of the machines I worked on would fill a basketball court. And it had only 256K of storage, that was made up of copper wire and tiny round magnets (core store).

After four years I applied to work overseas and moved with my firm to the United Arab Emirates and stayed there five years. The company then moved me to Germany, where I stayed for five years, and then America.

After twelve years of being overseas I came back to the UK and moved into sales – with the same company. I stayed with them a further thirteen years in sales.

My coaching

Then, in 2005 I struck out on my own, starting a business coaching business. And guess what? When I turned 60, I reinvented myself again, transforming into a high-growth Sales Consultant, expanding my client base and income.

In September 2024 I started another coaching business, this time to help psychics, healers, clairvoyants and so on. People who are collectively known as 'lightworkers'.

When I look back, I can see that this journey that you and I are on is all about embracing change and growth. And that is regardless of age. Now you and I need to fully give ourselves to forming a new life in this new age.

After decades of personal growth and reinvention, I've learned that thriving in later life requires embracing change head-on. But that doesn't mean there aren't challenges to navigate. As I steered through these changes, I became aware that every stage of life presents its own set of challenges. Turning 60 is no different, and while there are plenty of opportunities, there are also real concerns we must face head-on.

Challenges and realities

Let's not sugarcoat it – you know that life after 60 has its challenges. Ageism is still a real issue, and financial insecurity, health concerns, and social isolation can be significant hurdles. Ignoring these realities would be a disservice.

But here's the good news: you and I are in this together. Throughout this book, we'll explore these challenges head-on, looking at practical tools and resources to travel through them with empathy and openness. By acknowledging these obstacles, you and I can empower ourselves and others to overcome them and claim our rightful place in society.

Changing limiting beliefs

I would also love you to know that you can be wealthy after you reach the age of 60. Our society seems to teach us that creating wealth is difficult. And we are led to believe that if we make money, then someone else will be lacking. This is not true. I aim to show you in this book that there is unlimited wealth on our planet and you can create as much of it as you would like.

This universe is a giving universe that wants us all to succeed. We are all here to reach our potential and live in abundance. We will probe deeper into our own belief system, what influences it and how we can change it to earn what we want.

The shift

I am also setting out to prepare you for a paradigm shift. Interestingly, whilst we are both going through our personal shift –

so planet Earth is going through a shift. The guidance in this book, coupled with the positive changes that are starting to happen in the world, will help you achieve whatever you want.

This isn't just about personal transformation; it's a call to action to dismantle ageism and create a world where everyone, regardless of age, can thrive.

You see, ageing isn't something to be feared. It's a new chapter, a chance for you to explore new passions, to learn new things, and to live life on your own terms. It's about breaking free from the limitations imposed by societal expectations.

Let's challenge the idea that older adults are less capable, less valuable, or less relevant. Let's celebrate the wisdom, experience, and unique contributions that come with age. In this time of change, we can help to create a society that values diversity in all its forms, including age diversity.

So, let's embark on this journey together. Let's challenge our own beliefs about ageing and inspire others to do the same. Together, we can create a world where age is seen as a source of strength, not a limitation. It's time to embrace the beauty of ageing and redefine what it means to grow old.

Potential adventures ahead

You and I have reached a point in life where we've seen firsthand the joys and challenges that come with ageing. And we both know; it's not all doom and gloom. In fact, it can be an incredibly rewarding time.

This personal self-help guide is meant to help you navigate the ups and downs of your later years. I want to provide you with the tools, knowledge, and inspiration to live your best life.

I have already spoken about my own journey to reach the age of 70. I left school without anything to show for eleven years in state education. Now at 70 I'm running my own consultancy business and involved in dozens of things and I am still climbing mountains. I'm mentally active, physically active and wish to work until my last breath because what I do is helping people. I say all of that because I have a very strong belief in myself and, as we will cover later, I believe that is the most fundamental thing we must have. I have always believed I was invincible and this has gone a long way to keep me hale and hearty.

Anyway, while I can't turn back the clock, I can offer insights and advice that might make your journey a little easier. Some of what I share might surprise you, might even make you think, "I wish I had known this sooner." But the good news is, it's never too late to start making changes.

Also, some of things covered here might seem a little 'whacky' and I would just ask you to take it in with an open mind and ask yourself, "What if?" What if we are all capable of much more than we currently perceive?

This book is about more than just surviving retirement; it's about thriving. It's about discovering new passions, building meaningful relationships, and embracing the unique opportunities that come with age.

I'll be honest, there will be challenges. Health issues, financial concerns, and emotional ups and downs are all part of the experience. But I promise you, with the right mindset and strategies, you can overcome these obstacles and create a life that is fulfilling and rewarding.

So, let's dive in. Together, we'll explore topics like physical health, mental well-being, financial planning, and personal growth. We'll discuss the importance of staying active, maintaining a healthy diet, and seeking social connections. We'll also explore the power of positive thinking, how to manifest what you want, mindfulness, and personal development.

By the end of this book, you'll be armed with the knowledge, resources, and inspiration to rewrite your own narrative of ageing. You'll discover that life truly does begin at 60, not as a fixed starting point, but as an ongoing journey of self-discovery, growth, and boundless possibilities.

My motto for life: - Just Do It – is something I started saying in 1976, way before Nike!

Chapter 1 – Myth vs Reality

"An aged man is but a paltry thing. A tattered coat upon a stick."

W.B. Yeats, Sailing to Byzantium

A fresh start at 60: offering possibilities

There's a big difference between growing older and growing old. One is a natural process, a fact of life. The other is a **mindset**. It's about how we approach this new stage in our lives. So, let's challenge some of those old ideas about ageing. Let's break down a few myths and discover the exciting possibilities that come with experience.

Subjects in this chapter:

- Ageing is "all in the mind"
- Ageism – the invisible barrier
- Embracing the silver lining
- Our beliefs shape our reality
- Getting old in different parts of the world

First, a few of the myths of ageing

Ageing is a natural part of life, and it's accompanied by a host of myths and misconceptions. Let's explore the reality of ageing.

Myth 1: Ageing is inevitable decline

While it's true that some physical changes occur with age, it's important to remember that ageing does not have to mean decline. With proper care and attention, you can maintain a high quality of life well into your later years. Also, we need to be aware that the term itself, "later years", is a moving reference, since we are living longer Regular exercise, a healthy diet, and adequate sleep can help you stay physically and mentally fit.

Myth 2: You're too old to learn new things

The brain is incredibly adaptable, and it's never too late to learn something new. Whether it's a new language, a musical instrument, or a hobby, engaging in mentally stimulating activities can help keep your mind sharp and active. Were you like me, listening to all that fantastic music in the 60's and 70's? Well, I picked up the guitar later in life and now I get a huge amount of pleasure from playing and singing along to my old favourites. I love how it makes me feel.

Myth 3: Retirement means boredom

Retirement doesn't have to be a time of inactivity. There are countless opportunities to stay engaged and active, from volunteering to traveling to pursuing new hobbies and meeting new people. You could be doing something you are passionate about. That might mean starting a new business. More on that in Chapter 6.

Myth 4: Ageing means losing your independence

With proper planning and support, it's possible to maintain independence well into old age. Consider options like home care or assisted living to ensure you have the support you need to live comfortably and safely.

Myth 5: Ageing is a lonely time

While it's true that some people may experience loneliness as they age, it's important to remember that you're not alone. There are many ways to connect with others, from joining social groups to volunteering to using technology to stay in touch with loved ones.

Myth 6: Ageing means giving up on your dreams

It's never too late to pursue your dreams. Whether it's traveling the world, starting a business, or learning a new skill, age should not be a barrier. Neither should finance – and we will speak about that in Chapter 5 and Chapter 6.

Both you and I have lived through some colossal changes in the world. More than most, we can appreciate that anything is possible when we focus on our ambitions.

Myth 7: Ageing is a burden to others

Many older adults contribute significantly to their communities and the lives of others. Ageing can be a time of wisdom, experience, and giving back. We who are approaching or are in retirement can stay fit and healthy, making us a bonus in our families and our communities.

Please just keep in mind that if we **do** have issues (like mobility) our younger relatives and friends might be trying to help us in ways that we think will be a burden to them. Try to be aware of their good intentions and work with them. Start by listening to them and keep an open mind. Learn to accept the help offered by others, if you do really need it.

Myth 8: Ageing is synonymous with illness

While it's true that the risk of certain health conditions increases with age, it's important to remember that ageing doesn't mean you're destined for illness. By taking care of your health, you can reduce your risk of chronic diseases and enjoy a healthy, active life. We will talk more about this, for now just remember that you are in control of your body and not a 'slave' to it. If your mind is dwelling on poverty, that is what you will create.

Myth 9: Ageing is the end of your love life

Love and intimacy can be a fulfilling part of life at any age. There are many ways to maintain a healthy and satisfying relationship, even as you age.

Myth 10: Ageing is a time for regret

Instead of dwelling on the past, focus on the present and the future. Embrace the opportunities that come with ageing and make the most of your later years. You could perceive it as a time for making amends with people because the more relationships you have at our age, the less time you will spend ‘naval gazing’ about the past.

As with all of these myths, they are only true if you **believe** them. Later we will discover how important our internal thoughts are and we will have an exercise to show you how you can become what you want and who you want.

Ageing is a natural part of life, and it's an opportunity for growth and fulfilment. By challenging these myths and embracing the realities of ageing, we can live our best lives, no matter our age.

I am here to point out that reaching 60 can be a whole exciting new chapter in your life and that we need to stay as positive as we can be in mind and spirit.

There was a time in our recent history when people reached 60 and they simply 'faded away.' This was partly due to life expectancy realities. If you worked from age 16 to age 60, it was most likely in a physically demanding job - from labouring in fields and factories to intensive manual trades. Consequently, people were understandably worn out after over four decades of such exertion under their belts.

Retirement often meant a sharp decline in activity levels. The transition from a structured work environment to the unstructured freedom of retirement could be disorienting. Many found themselves struggling with a sense of purpose and identity. The social isolation that often accompanies retirement could exacerbate feelings of loneliness and depression.

However, significant societal and economic changes have transformed the landscape of retirement. Increased life expectancy, coupled with advancements in healthcare, have allowed people to live longer, healthier lives. The shift from a predominantly manufacturing-based economy to a service-based one has led to a wider range of job opportunities for older adults.

The rise of technology has connected people in ways that were unimaginable just a few decades ago. Social media platforms, video conferencing, and online communities have made it easier than ever to stay connected with friends and family, regardless of distance.

As a result, retirement is no longer synonymous with inactivity and isolation. Many older adults are embracing this new phase of life with enthusiasm, pursuing hobbies, traveling, volunteering, and even starting new businesses. Retirement can be a time of personal growth, discovery, and fulfilment.

It's important to recognise that the experience of retirement varies greatly from person to person. Some may find the transition seamless, while others may face challenges. However, with the right mindset and support, it is possible to embrace retirement as a positive and fulfilling experience.

My first pension scheme

I remember joining the pension scheme with ICL when I started as a computer engineer. I was 23 years old and a pension seemed as far away as Jupiter. When I reviewed their data, I was startled to see that only 3% of the people paying into the scheme actually lived long enough to receive their hard-earned pension benefits. That's an impressively profitable figure for the pension fund managers with so much accumulated capital, but it made me wonder if I had chosen the right career path with such grim life expectancy statistics staring me in the face. And this was a job where I was repairing electronic equipment in a clean, air-conditioned environment – far from life-threatening! But those dismal numbers were likely standard for that era.

Thankfully, the tides have shifted dramatically since those days. I've now enjoyed over a decade of receiving my company pension benefits - a reality that was seemingly improbable according to those aged statistics from my youth. Through a confluence of factors like improved workplace conditions, greater health awareness, and robust medical advances, life expectancy has risen compared to generations past.

So, you'd imagine that with better employment standards, people living longer, and heightened understanding around nutrition, exercise, and mental wellbeing, we would have an actively thriving population of joyful 60-plus individuals making the most of their golden years, right? Well, this is frequently not the reality we encounter.

Ageism: The invisible barrier

Instead, once we cross that symbolic 60-year threshold, we often find ourselves increasingly "greyed out" of cultural relevance—overlooked, undervalued, and sidelined from many of society's mainstream narratives and conversations. We become easily dismissible, our wealth of hard-earned wisdom and life experience too quickly discarded like an outdated fashion trend.

This phenomenon (let's call it what it is – ageism), is as pervasive as it is insidious. It manifests in subtle and covert ways, from age-based discrimination in the workplace to the assumption that older adults are less capable or relevant. It's a bias that can have a profound impact on our self-esteem, our mental health, and even our physical well-being.

Ageism often stems from societal stereotypes and misconceptions about ageing. We're often portrayed as grumpy, out of touch, or a burden on society. These stereotypes are not only harmful but also inaccurate. Older adults are as diverse as any other group, with a wide range of interests, skills, and experiences.

The consequences of ageism can be far-reaching. It can lead to financial hardship, social isolation, and a decline in overall quality of life. When we are seen as irrelevant or disposable, it can erode our sense of purpose and belonging.

It's time to challenge these harmful stereotypes and create a society that values and respects people of all ages. We need to advocate for policies that protect older adults from discrimination and promote their active participation in society. We also need to foster a culture of intergenerational respect and understanding.

To be clear, I do not wish to have you think it's all 'their' fault. I mean those people not yet at our level of maturity. You also have to take some responsibility if you are an old curmudgeon. I want you to be pleasant and engage with your juniors because there is so much you can help them with. Remember to smile when you engage with 'them'!

By challenging ageism, we can create a world where everyone, regardless of age, feels valued, included, and empowered. It's a world where wisdom and experience are celebrated, not dismissed. It's a world where ageing is seen as a natural and positive part of life.

Compounding this marginalisation are the startling numbers of 60-plus individuals grappling with deteriorating mental and physical health, financial strains forcing an austere existence, overwhelming feelings of loneliness and isolation, and challenges with stress, anxiety, and purpose. Getting 'old' has become a foreboding state to be avoided rather than an enriching, vitalising next chapter of life to be embraced wholeheartedly.

While ageism is a reality, it's not a sentence for us to live a lesser life. In fact, we are the creators of our reality and we will cover more on that in the next chapter.

Embracing the silver lining

I'm here to reject those disempowering narratives and societal norms! Because the reality is, with some strategic lifestyle adaptations to realign with our core needs as we age, there is no reason we can't joyfully thrive and reach new levels of fulfilment, well-being, and growth in our 60s, 70s, 80s and beyond.

One key to ageing gracefully is to prioritise self-care. This doesn't mean splurging on expensive treatments or products. It simply means taking the time to nourish your body, mind, and soul. Ensure you're getting enough sleep, eating a balanced diet, and engaging in regular physical activity. Even a brisk walk or a gentle yoga session can do wonders.

Mental well-being is just as important. Cultivate a positive mindset by practicing gratitude, mindfulness, or meditation. Surround yourself with uplifting influences, whether it's inspiring books, uplifting music, or positive role models. And don't be afraid to seek professional help if you're struggling with mental health issues.

Social connections are another vital aspect of ageing well. Nurture your existing relationships and make an effort to meet new people. Join clubs, groups, or volunteer organisations to expand your social circle. Human connection is a powerful antidote to loneliness and can provide a sense of purpose and belonging.

Finally, don't be afraid to embrace change. As we age, our priorities and interests may shift. Be open to new experiences, learn new skills, and explore different avenues of fulfilment. Whether it's traveling, taking up a new hobby, or pursuing a lifelong dream, embracing change can keep life exciting and fulfilling. And if you are wondering how you might do this, we will delve into having the finances you want, staying active and healthy (both physically and mentally) and keeping a positive focus.

Ageing is not a race against time; it's a journey of self-discovery and growth. By making conscious choices and embracing the unique opportunities that come with each stage of life, we can thrive and age gracefully. So, let's shed the negative stereotypes and redefine what it means to grow old. The best is yet to come!

Imagine a future phase of your life with good health, overflowing with purpose, deepening wisdom, novel adventures, and bliss. A time when you feel more fully alive and engaged with each experience than ever before. A passage where each day beckons you into a playground of learning, creating and connecting.

This. Is. Possible.

OK, I'm ready to change!

So how do you grasp these changes and turn them to your advantage? How do you shake off society's beliefs, fears, and stories that no longer serve you so we can reclaim the sort of living that an exceptional life over sixty will give you?

Let's be clear – you have the power to create a life with sound health, meaningful connections, purpose, abundance, regardless of what culturally inherited mindsets and stories might have you believe. You will need to embrace some empowering daily mindset practices and collected wisdom that comes from my own journey so far. Some people call this manifestation.

Humbug Alert!

I'm not promising a magical cure-all for every challenge you'll face as you approach or navigate retirement. Life is full of twists and turns, and there will undoubtedly be obstacles along the way. However, I can assure you this: if you commit to the insights and practices contained in this book, the "very much alive" way of living that emerges will make it one of the greatest chapters of your life.

This book is more than just a guide; it's an invitation. It's an invitation to explore the boundless possibilities that await you in this new stage of life. It's a chance to redefine what it means to grow old gracefully and with purpose.

By embracing the principles outlined here, you'll discover the power of self-care, the joy of lifelong learning, the importance of social connections, and the beauty of living in the present moment. You'll learn to cultivate a positive mindset, manage stress effectively, and find meaning in every day.

Retirement is an opportunity to explore new passions, to make a difference in the world, and to rediscover the joy of living. By embracing the "very much alive" lifestyle, you'll unlock the potential that lies within you and create a retirement that is truly extraordinary.

Redefining our expectations of later life

As we discussed earlier, society's outdated views on ageing can limit us – If we let them. So now, let's focus on how we can rewrite that story for ourselves.

When you believe that this is a time of decline, limitations, and fading dreams, then, for you at least – it will be!

However, when you believe that you are on the threshold to a vibrant and dynamic new chapter in your life – it will be!

I believe (now that I am at a more 'mature' age) that it is **all in our minds**. How we think and how we feel will determine how we live. This is how the universe works. I understand this not just from studying the make-up of the world but from my own life experiences. So called "New Age" philosophy prescribes to this – but so does quantum physics!

I would like to shatter the myths surrounding ageing and empower you to embrace the vast possibilities that lie ahead for you. So, before we go any further, let me expand on that statement by sharing my latest philosophy of life.

The Quantum Leap: how our beliefs shape reality

Before I delve into the quantum world, I want you to know that what I am going cover here is possibly hard for you to believe. All I ask of you is to simply ask, "What if?"

What if this really is how the world works? What if my thoughts and beliefs are creating the world in which I'm living? I ask that you take time to contemplate the prospect that you are the creator of your own destiny.

Over the last few years, I've been on a personal journey to understand the mechanics of the universe. It's been a fascinating exploration, one that has led me to a very interesting intersection: the point where spirituality and science intertwine.

I've come to understand that our belief systems play a pivotal role in shaping our lives. Our thoughts, our emotions, and our negativity all contribute to the experiences we encounter. Quantum scientists now have a far greater understanding about how our belief system creates our future. This includes the thoughts we have, the negativity we hold and the illnesses we create in ourselves. It might sound strange, even counterintuitive, but it's a concept rooted in quantum physics.

In the quantum world, everything is potential, a sea of possibilities. It's only when we observe or interact with these possibilities that they solidify into reality. Our intentions, our beliefs, act as filters, selecting specific outcomes from this quantum soup.

Our subconscious mind, the powerful engine beneath the surface, is the key to this process. It's constantly listening, interpreting our thoughts and feelings, and translating them into physical manifestations. What you tell yourself becomes your truth, shaping your reality.

This means we're not passive victims of circumstance. We're active creators, shaping our own destinies through our thoughts and beliefs. This isn't about wishful thinking or magical thinking;

it's about understanding the underlying principles that govern our existence.

It's a profound concept. It places the responsibility for our lives squarely in our own hands. It's a call to examine our beliefs, to challenge our limiting thoughts, and to cultivate a more positive mindset. So, what are you choosing to create today? Because whether you realise it or not, you're already shaping your future.

To bring this concept down to everyday life, let's look at a simple example of how our thoughts influence our physical state, perhaps an example with which you can relate more easily.

Physical manifestation of a thought

How we think and how we feel determines our personal reality. Let me try to give you an example of how powerful our thoughts and emotions really are – thoughts and emotions powerful enough to force a change in our physical body.

Ever noticed how your face turns red when you're embarrassed? It's a fascinating example of how our minds can literally change our bodies to an altered state and then change them back again. Let's break down what's happening here.

First, our conscious mind registers an awkward situation. Maybe we've said something silly or stumbled over our words. Our subconscious, ever the problem-solver, then kicks into action. It starts sending out signals throughout our body, like a tiny conductor directing an orchestra.

These signals trigger the release of neuropeptides, tiny chemical messengers that travel through our bloodstream. Some of these neuropeptides head straight for our blood vessels, causing them to dilate. This increased blood flow expands the small veins in our face and this is what makes our cheeks 'flush'.

But it's not just about the blood vessels. Our subconscious also influences other bodily functions. It might make our heart race, our palms sweat or even cause our knees to shake. Our body is physically reacting to the emotional state our mind has created.

Then, when the embarrassment has passed, the emotion subsides and the body reverts to its original state.

It's a fascinating reminder of the interconnectedness of our minds and bodies. Our thoughts and feelings can have a profound impact on our physical appearance. So, the next time you feel yourself blushing, take a moment to appreciate the incredible complexity of the human body. And please take time to contemplate how your thoughts are shaping your future – even as you read this.

The power of intention

Our intentions, whether conscious or subconscious, act as powerful magnets, attracting experiences that align with them. If we focus on lack, negativity, or fear, we're more likely to manifest those experiences in our lives. Conversely, by cultivating positive intentions, we can attract abundance, joy, and fulfilment.

That intent is set by our subconscious mind. So, what we tell ourselves is 'listened to' by our subconscious and then matter is created to match that belief. What we tell ourselves becomes our truth.

Consider the placebo effect. When people believe a fake treatment will work, they often experience real benefits. This demonstrates the power of the mind to influence physical outcomes. Similarly, your beliefs about yourself can shape your self-esteem, your relationships, and even your health.

Placebo example

Further to this, there was an experiment conducted in the USA with Parkinson's patients. Parkinson's occurs when the brain no longer produces its own dopamine. That means the neural pathways from the brain to other parts of the body become less effective and, over time, ineffective. Hence the Parkinson's tremor that a lot of Parkinson's patients have – the patient can't send signals from the brain down to the hands to take control and stop them shaking.

A group of Parkinson's patients were called in and told there was an amazing new drug that cured Parkinson's and each member of the group was given instruction and the wonder-drug and sent home. When they returned after some time, there was a percentage of them that had no Parkinson's symptoms.

This, smaller group, was then examined and it was found that – in all of them – they were now producing their own dopamine! Then, they brought back the whole group that were involved in the experiment and explained that they were all given a fake drug and they were being tested in regard to the placebo effect, not a new wonder drug.

Within a few days, those Parkinson's patients who had started using their own dopamine producing cells again all stopped producing dopamine.

When that subset of patients whose symptoms disappeared believed that they had taken a cure, their subconscious mind fell into step with the latest belief and switched on the dopamine producing cells. Then, when they were told of the placebo experiment, their subconscious mind was told, “no, go back, we were tricked, there isn’t a wonder cure.” And it switched off the dopamine producing cells once more.

What we believe about ourselves each day is creating the life we live each day.

To make big changes in our lives, <u>we need to believe those changes are already in place and then the subconscious will create them.</u>

To be clear, when I am suggesting that the subconscious mind is in control of whether we are sick or not, I am not suggesting the patient is to blame. All of our subconscious minds are working the same way.

It is our perception – our belief – that determines our outcome.

I say this to give people hope. Not to castigate but to liberate.

The role of emotions

Our emotions are another powerful force shaping our reality. Negative emotions like anger, fear, and resentment can create a toxic environment that attracts more negativity. Positive emotions like love, joy, and gratitude, on the other hand, can create a more harmonious and fulfilling life.

The key is to become aware of our thoughts and emotions and to consciously choose those that serve us. By cultivating positive emotions and beliefs, we can shift our vibrational frequency and attract more positive experiences.

The 'Law of Attraction'

While the concept might seem simplistic, it's grounded in scientific principles. The law of attraction states that like attracts like. If we focus on positive thoughts and emotions, we're more likely to attract positive experiences.

This doesn't mean that problems or challenges won't arise. Life is full of ups and downs. However, by understanding the power of our minds, we can navigate these challenges with greater resilience and grace.

So, how can we apply these principles to our daily lives?

Become aware of your thoughts: Pay attention to the thoughts running through your mind. Are they positive or negative?

Challenge negative thoughts: When you notice a negative thought, question its validity. Is it really true? Is there another way to look at the situation?

Visualise your desired outcomes: Create mental images of the life you want to live. The more vivid and detailed your visualisations, the more powerful they will be. As you visualise, feel it in the present tense, that you are already living that dream life.

Practice gratitude: Focus on the things you're grateful for. Gratitude can shift your perspective and attract more positive experiences.

Surround yourself with positivity: Spend time with people who uplift and inspire you. Limit your exposure to negativity.

By understanding the power of our minds, we can take control of our lives and create the reality we desire. It's a journey of self-discovery, self-improvement, and empowerment.

You are the creator of your own reality. Choose your thoughts wisely and watch your world transform.

We are responsible for what happens in our lives and we create our future based on our thoughts and our feelings. What we think and how we feel creates our experiences. We will re-visit this in more detail later in Chapter 2 – Physical Wellbeing.

Manifesting your wishes

During my recent 'journey of discovery', I studied hypnosis and I was so interested that I enrolled in classes and now I'm a qualified hypnotherapist. I can see first-hand the power of hypnosis. One thing I find extremely interesting is that a person cannot be hypnotised – it's all self-hypnosis. The person allows the hypnotist to lead them down the path of where the person being hypnotised wishes to go. When actually, they could do the same thing by themselves.

People believe in the 'power' of the hypnotist and yet, whenever we focus internally we can use self-hypnosis. This follows the natural way the mind works (what we think about, we bring about).

We can use this internal 'power' we have to our advantage. We can use natural hypnosis to set new beliefs.

Here is an exercise you can do. For only five minutes a day, focus your attention on one simple statement. Repeat your statement the whole time while you focus on it. You can say the statement aloud if you are alone or repeat it in your head if needs be. Think about times in your past when this statement was true. It also helps when you think of the present moment and see yourself as having this statement come true. Feel it, as if it has already come to pass in your present.

Doing this exercise means you are using the present moment to change your internal beliefs for the future.

When you have completed the five minutes, there is no need to dwell on it and no need to repeat it throughout the day. Do this exercise every day for one month and you will notice a difference.

Example exercise:

Let's say you have issues regarding using the toilet. This can be constipation or diarrhoea, swings between both extremes or accidents before getting there. It can be similar issues with your bladder.

So, we can make the statement, "I am really grateful that my bladder and bowels are working perfectly." Now, repeat that aloud or inside your head for five minutes. Whilst you are going through the words, think about a previous time when you had no such issues. Think about how that felt. Really feel it. You were free to live your life and not be hindered by how close you were to the bathroom. Keep the repetition going. If you run out of memories of blissful 'bladder and bowel perfection' then add in feelings of how it is now that your bladder and bowels are working sweetly. Feel it as if it has already happened. It's very important that you feel the emotion here.

After five minutes, leave it for that day and repeat the next day. Within one month of following this exercise and really feeling that everything has improved, you will notice a positive change.

We can use this same exercise to manifest other positive changes in your life. Whether that's increasing your wealth, improving your health or improving your mental wellbeing.

The physical side of how this works is explained more in the next chapter.

When things don't go our way we become stressed

Choosing your thoughts wisely is a great lead-in to how we create a lot of our mental anxieties.

You are creating your own reality every day. You 'paint the picture' of a world through your own eyes. More correctly, it's through your own mind. Your mind presents you with images that reflect how you see the world.

Now, I know this from experience but it has only become apparent to me recently that this is causing me anxiety.

You see, the world my mind conjures up for me each day is the world **I believe** exists. That world is unique to me. I am correct in thinking it exists because it is my own 'work' and it is how I see things – and therefore how my subconscious mind is presenting things to me. I am not suggesting that this is by any means the **correct world**, merely that it is **my world**.

Now, consider that is the same for every human on the planet.

Everyone one else's world is created in the same way. Each day, every individual is conjuring up what **they believe** their world to be. And, because they believe it, so it is created.

The ‘conflict’ arises when we interact with another human. We need to understand that the other person has ‘painted a picture’ of their world – and it is different to ours. When the other person does or says something that runs counter to our picture of the world, we become very uncomfortable. If we go down the rabbit-hole of trying to interpret their actions or words in our own terms it can lead to anxiety.

For example, let’s use a driving allegory. When we let someone into the flow of traffic and they do not indicate their appreciation in any way. When we discover that someone has parked so far over into our parking bay that we find it difficult to park and then get out of the car. When a driver fails to signal at a junction or when they simply crawl along in front, taking in the view. When we are signalling our intent to move into a street parking slot from the other side of the road and then someone comes towards us and pulls into the parking slot.

What causes adrenaline and cortisol to start pumping round our system are thoughts like, “I wouldn’t do that. What an idiot. How selfish.” We might feel slighted. We might feel ignored. We feel badly done to. But that is in “our world”. That view of what’s right and wrong has been shaped over our lifetime and we do not like it when things do not go how we expect. So, we project our negativity onto the alleged perpetrator and we work ourselves up into stress.

We become upset and then start to justify ‘our’ thoughts over everyone else’s and keep telling ourselves that ‘our’ thoughts are a true reflection of the world. Add to that, the fact that we make the opposing person ‘the enemy’, then we can justify to ourselves that we are correct in becoming angry (or call it indignant, annoyed, upset, outraged – they are all levels of anger). Then our attacks, be they verbal, physical or simply remain in our head, become warranted. We assign our own 'moral' judgement to everything and then, by definition, the other person falls short of this. We believe we hold the moral high ground.

Unbeknown to us, the other person, this 'spawn of the devil', is completely oblivious. They have done exactly what's expected in **their world**. They will not understand why we might feel slighted. They do not need to signal their thanks, they do not need to worry about taking up more of their share of the parking lot, they do not consider it useful to use traffic signals or move out of the way if they are slowing traffic down or worry about who was first to a vacant parking space. They have had no need to fire up their adrenal glands because everything is going to plan for them.

And rest assured, **we** will be doing things that rub other people up the wrong way.

I work on my internal thinking when (if) I catch myself thinking like this. First is the realisation that I am expecting things to go the way I map them out in my world. Then the understanding that the other person is doing **exactly the same as me**. Then the appreciation of the other person's lifetime experiences and biases that are shaping their world. Then the calming thought that I have not been slighted or ignored and that the uncomfortable feeling I'm having is my own ego and there is no need to continue – so I LET IT GO.

If another driver cuts out in front of us and then slows to a crawl while we are driving to work, we will want to tell someone about it, through our own lens. We will be indignant that we were 'badly done to' by some stranger. Then we will carry that 'negativity' for most of the morning, re-creating the 'crime against us' and pumping up adrenaline and cortisol. This sets our day off on a negative basis, which can set the scene for a stress-filled day.

Because everything else that happens, good or bad, will be influenced by our mood.

Because things do not go the way we expect, we do not need to stress. **We can just breathe and let go**.

Getting old is not all bad

So, yes, we create a lot of problems for ourselves. But now that we have seen how our lives are being created, we can also see that **you** are the only person responsible for **your** problems and **you** can make changes. And getting old gives you liberties. You can create the life you want and go on the adventures you want and people will simply say, "Oh, ignore him, he's just old." You can just laugh as you scoot past them on your roller-skates.

It's like being a kid again, only with better shoes! You don't have to follow the rules. You don't have to impress anyone. You can be as weird and wonderful as you like. Want to learn to tango? Do it. Fancy taking up skydiving? Go for it. Who's going to stop you?

Of course, there are challenges. Health issues might creep in, and loneliness can be a sneaky visitor. But these are challenges, not roadblocks. They're opportunities to discover new strengths, to build resilience, and to find unexpected sources of joy.

Remember that amazing feeling of freedom you had as a teenager? Well, it's back, and it's even better this time around. You've got the wisdom, the experience, and the confidence to make the most of it. You are not just surviving, you are thriving. This is your time to redefine life on your terms – so grab it with both hands and run with it!

So, let's embrace this stage of life with open arms. Let's fill our days with laughter, learning, and love. Let's redefine what it means to grow old. Because, let's face it, you are writing the script for this period, and it's time to make it a bestseller.

Now, that's not to say it's always easy. There will be days when you feel tired, or maybe a bit lost. That's okay. Everyone feels like that sometimes. But remember, you've got this. You've been through a lot, and you've come out stronger on the other side.

So, let's make this the best chapter yet. You are writing your own story, so why not fill it with adventure, friendship, and a whole lot of fun. After all, you only get one go at this, so let's make it count.

A global view of ageing

Turning 60 is a milestone and I'm happy to say, it's not the same in every country.

Yes, it's a time of reflection, accomplishment, and maybe even a few well-deserved grey hairs. But how different cultures celebrate and support their elders can be as diverse as the spices in an Arabic souk.

East Asia: Reverence and wisdom

In many East Asian cultures, elders are treated with deep respect, thanks to Confucian traditions. Turning 60 in China is a big deal—it's like a second birth, a fresh start! A time to shed past burdens and embrace a new chapter. Celebrations often involve large family gatherings, elaborate meals, and the presentation of red envelopes filled with lucky money. Respect for elders is deeply ingrained; younger family members readily offer assistance and prioritise their elders' needs.

Japan takes a similar approach. Reaching 60, particularly for men, is called "kanreki," a significant life transition. Special ceremonies are held, and families wear red clothing to ward off evil spirits. Elders are revered for their wisdom, often holding positions of authority within families and communities.

Latin America: Strength and vibrancy

Latin American cultures celebrate ageing with a zest for life. In Mexico, turning 60 is known as "las seis décadas" (the six decades). Families often throw lively parties with music, dancing, and traditional foods. Elders are seen as pillars of strength, with their stories and experiences passed down through generations.

Similarly, in Brazil, 60 is a time for joy and celebration. Families throw "festas de aniversário" (birthday parties) filled with music, laughter, and delicious food. Elders are highly respected for their resilience and often play a vital role in childcare, offering love and guidance to younger generations.

Sub-Saharan Africa: A celebration of ancestors

In many Sub-Saharan African cultures, elders are considered living ancestors, embodying the wisdom and guidance of past generations. Reaching 60 is often seen as a significant achievement, marked by ceremonies and rituals that reflect the community's respect and appreciation.

For instance, the Maasai people of Kenya celebrate elders with a "sentetu" ceremony, where men transition from warriors to respected elders. In Ghana, reaching 60 is called "adwoa kese," meaning "big Wednesday." Elaborate ceremonies are held, with families offering gifts and expressing gratitude to the elder for their contributions to the community.

The West: Redefining retirement

Our own cultures traditionally viewed retirement as a time for leisure and relaxation. However, with increasing lifespans, many individuals are seeking more purpose beyond traditional retirement models. Senior centres are evolving to offer educational courses, social activities, and volunteer opportunities.

The concept of "active retirement" is gaining traction, encouraging older adults to stay engaged physically, mentally, and socially. Technology is also playing a role, with online communities and communication platforms connecting elders across geographical boundaries.

Embracing a global mosaic of ageing

It's fascinating to see how different cultures view and celebrate ageing.

These diverse perspectives remind us that ageing is a universal experience, but the way we approach it varies greatly. By understanding these cultural differences, we can appreciate the richness and diversity of human experience.

As we age, it's important to honour our own traditions and cultural heritage. It's also a wonderful opportunity to foster intergenerational connections. Spending time with younger generations can keep us young at heart and help them learn valuable lessons from our experiences.

Here are some resources for further exploration:

HelpAge International: www.helpage.org (A global organization advocating for the rights of older people)

National Institute on Aging: www.nia.nih.gov (US government resource on ageing research and information)

The Global Ageing Network: www.un.org/en/global-issues/ageing (A UN initiative promoting the well-being of older persons)

Ageing is a universal experience. By celebrating the wisdom and contributions of our elders, and learning from diverse cultural perspectives, we can create a world where everyone can flourish, regardless of age.

Getting ready

Now that we've seen how different cultures view ageing, let's turn inward and explore what we can do to take charge of our own ageing experience.

So, we know there are some challenges and opportunities that come with ageing. We've seen how our mindset plays a crucial role in shaping our experiences. Now a quick summary of the importance of physical, mental, emotional, and spiritual well-being.

Physical health

As we age, it's natural for our bodies to change. However, with proper care and attention, we can maintain a high quality of life. Regular exercise, a balanced diet, and adequate sleep are essential for physical health.

Exercise: Even moderate exercise can have significant benefits. Consider activities like walking, swimming, or yoga.

Nutrition: A balanced diet rich in fruits, vegetables, whole grains, and lean proteins can help prevent chronic diseases and maintain energy levels.

Sleep: Aim for around six hours of quality sleep each night. Establishing a consistent sleep routine can improve sleep quality.

Mental health

Mental health is just as important as physical health. Engaging in mentally stimulating activities, practicing mindfulness, and seeking social connections can all contribute to a healthy mind.

Keep your brain active with puzzles, games, or learning new skills.

Mindfulness practices like meditation and deep breathing can help reduce stress and improve focus.

Spending time with loved ones and building new friendships can provide emotional support and a sense of belonging.

Personal relationships

As we age, our relationships become even more precious. Friends and family are the anchors that keep us grounded, the shoulders we can lean on, and the partners in crime for life's adventures.

You've made it to 60 or beyond so we know you've experienced a lot. You've faced challenges, celebrated triumphs, and grown as a person. Having people by your side who understand and support you through it all is invaluable.

Strong relationships can also have a positive impact on our physical and mental health. Studies have shown that people with strong social connections are less likely to experience depression, loneliness, and even some physical ailments.

So, make time for the people you love. Reach out, share stories, and create new memories together. It's not just about the quantity of relationships, but the quality. A few close friends who truly care about you can make all the difference in the world.

Of course, now that you and I are at our current level of maturity, it's natural for our social circles to change. Friends move away, some face health challenges, and life takes its course. If we aren't intentional about making new connections, our contact list can shrink, leaving us more isolated. But relationships don't have to be limited by age. Being open to new friendships—including with younger people—can bring fresh energy, perspectives, and joy into our lives.

Younger friends can introduce us to new ideas, technologies, and ways of thinking. In turn, we offer them wisdom, life experiences, and a sense of stability. These intergenerational connections can be deeply rewarding for both sides. Whether it's bonding over a shared hobby, volunteering together, or simply having meaningful conversations, age becomes irrelevant when friendships are built on mutual respect and genuine connection.

To expand your circle, consider joining local clubs, attending community events, or engaging with neighbours. Say yes to invitations, initiate conversations, and be open to new experiences. Friendships thrive when nurtured, regardless of age. By welcoming younger people into our lives, we ensure that our world remains full of laughter, companionship, and fresh perspectives—keeping us engaged and connected at any stage of life.

We will dive deeper into personal relationships in Chapter 4.

Emotional well-being

Being able to acknowledge, understand, and manage emotions effectively is essential for a fulfilling life. Developing emotional intelligence, managing stress, and seeking support when needed can help you navigate life's challenges.

Learn to identify and manage your emotions.

Practice relaxation techniques like deep breathing, yoga, or meditation.

Don't hesitate to reach out to friends, family, or mental health professionals when you need help.

Spiritual well-being

Spiritual well-being can provide a sense of purpose and meaning. Whether it's through religion, meditation, or simply spending time in nature, exploring your spiritual side can enrich your life.

Explore different spiritual paths to find what resonates with you.

Spending time in nature can be a powerful way to connect with your inner self.

Reflect on your values and purpose in life.

Financial planning

Financial security can provide peace of mind in later years. Creating a budget, saving for retirement, and seeking professional advice can help you achieve financial stability.

Track your income and expenses to create a budget that works for you.

Start saving for retirement early, even if it's a small amount.

Consult with a financial advisor to create a personalised retirement plan.

Wealth creation

Retirement doesn't mean the end of your journey. It's actually a great time to start a new adventure: wealth creation. Now, I know what you're thinking, "But I'm too old for that!" Well, think again. Age is just a number, and with the right mindset and strategies, you can create a sustainable income stream, even in your golden years.

Wealth creation isn't just about money; it's about freedom. It gives you the flexibility to do what you love, travel where you want, and live life on your own terms. It's about securing your future and providing for loved ones.

There are many ways to create wealth, from investing to starting a small business. It's about finding what works for you and your lifestyle. Whether you're interested in stocks, real estate, or creating a product or service, there are countless opportunities to explore.

Wealth creation is about setting goals, taking calculated risks, and learning from your experiences. So, why not give it a try? You might be surprised at what you can achieve.

Community involvement

Staying connected to your community can provide a sense of belonging and purpose. Volunteering, joining clubs, or participating in local events can help you meet new people and make a positive impact.

This is just a starting point. The key to thriving in later years is to find what works best for you. Experiment with different activities, listen to your body, and don't be afraid to try new things. By taking care of yourself physically, mentally, emotionally, and spiritually, you can create a fulfilling and vibrant life.

Later in the book we will be diving deeper into all of these areas and explore practical strategies for thriving in our later years.

Summary

Things have changed since the time of our parents retiring (for the better). Due to better healthcare provision, we are living longer and more healthy lives.

There are more opportunities open to us than there used to be and we can stay 'connected' more easily.

How we think and how we feel determines how we live.

If we think, 'poor me' and 'I'm frail' and 'I have no money', then that is the voice that is picked up by the subconscious and that exact scenario is created for us.

We've looked at ageing in different parts of the world and here in the UK we do not come out smelling of roses. And countries that place youthfulness and good looks before experience and intelligence also get low rankings.

My advice to you is to act as if you have been given a certain time left to live

In truth, we really do all have only so much time left. But when we get to our levels of maturity, we should live our lives more fully. Imagine the doctor told you there was only one more week. You would live that last week to the max! You would see your loved ones, complete your 'bucket list', set your affairs in order, forgive those that have 'trespassed against you' and everything else that people do when there is a short time left.

Well, **live like that now**. Read on and see how.

Chapter 2 - Physical Wellbeing

"Grow old along with me! The best is yet to be."

Rabbi Ben Ezra" by Robert Browning

I know there is a part of you that would like to simply skip this chapter. Right? There is a train of thought that goes something like – here we are, another 'poke in the eye' for me and a reminder to exercise and go on a diet.

But I'm doing OK aren't I? I haven't been sick in a while, I'm not the most 'stout' among my social group, I use the stairs rather than the escalator when I have time. This is all meant for the other people isn't it?

Most of us give ourselves permission to do nothing about our physical welfare. Believe me, you do not want to be dependent on the health service for them to deliver you long term care. Let us help the health service by taking our illnesses (a lot of it self-inflicted) out of their hands – and focus on our own physical wellbeing.

Subjects in this chapter:

- My experience of 70 years in this body
- We can decide whether or not we are healthy
- What we can do to improve our physical wellbeing

It's generally accepted that by the age of 60 we will be doing less exercise and that we will be suffering from at least a few ailments.

Those health issues can be something major like cardiovascular disease or arthritis, down to hearing loss or cataracts. It's what we've (kind of) come to expect. As we reach maturity, we seem to expect 'bits will drop off'. Sometimes literally!

This does not need to be the case. We can start to look after ourselves from any age. And, as we will discover, we are mostly affected by how we think.

My experience

As you know from the Foreword earlier, I was one of six children brought up on a council estate. Well, let me just say, that I was born in Middlesbrough – a challenging part of the world in the early 1950s. At the time I arrived in the world we still had the effects of the Second World War and were still affected by partial rationing. My parents were born just after the First World War and there was little change in those days from the Victorian era when children had to be "seen and not heard". So, they were ill-equipped to bring six children into the world and raise six responsible adults.

I had the general feeling of being taught to walk and talk and then being told to "sit down and shut up".

Eight humans in a small house inevitably caused 'conflict' and in our house, it was usually resolved with shouting and hitting. Physical violence was a common occurrence. And certainly, in my own personal case, there was not much love or compassion shown. As a child, I witnessed my mother being punched in the face and crying whilst my father stole money from her purse to buy alcohol. I mention this because domestic violence was common when I was a child and the authorities would not intervene in what they would consider an issue between a man and his wife. I also wanted to include it because there is a chance that you too witnessed behaviour like this when you were a child. I want you to know that you can forgive and let it go.

My father has been forgiven in his absence. To be fair to my parents, all of us children turned out well and went on to have families of our own. But thanks to that early life, when it comes to being in reasonable shape and active, I am fairly used to eating less and having to walk to places. It's just what we all did in northern England in the nineteen-fifties and sixties. Not much money for food and none at all for public transport.

We did not have a TV in the house until I was around ten years old. Every other electronic distraction was yet to be invented. As a child I would walk three miles to Eston Hills, wander around the moorland all day and then walk home again. When I left school at 16, I gained a position as an apprentice electrician and I had to walk two miles each day to work – and then the same home. I don't say this because I was anything special – everyone I knew was in this position.

As I grew older, I developed a love for walking. Possibly because I seemed to have endless energy and walking was second nature. I discovered Helvellyn in the Lake District when I was about nineteen and fell in love with mountains. I have tried to keep up that ability all through my life. When I turned seventy, I returned to Helvellyn just to see if I still could. The answer was yes. In that same year I walked the Yorkshire Three Peaks challenge, which is 26 miles and three mountains in one day. Keeping up my interest in nature and going for long walks has helped me stay in shape.

I have joined a gym (just once) when my wife wanted to attend every week and I thought I would support her. We both went on and off for about three years. Running on a machine was boring for me. So, I used to run to and from the gym, whilst my wife would drive and I would meet her there. On days when we were not going to the gym, I would also run for about an hour in our local area, in the countryside.

Tending to the garden is also something I have always been interested in. I love planting seeds or taking cuttings and seeing the unbelievable transformation that nature provides. I always think it's a miracle. I am reasonably good with my hands, so I do all my own repairs and DIY around the home. Both of these activities require bending and stretching and climbing ladders.

I also keep honeybees in my garden as a hobby. It's interest that has kept my mind active because no matter how many books you read about honeybees; you never have all the answers – because the bees don't read the same books! Keeping bees also requires physical bending and lifting, helping me to stay in shape.

That is it for the exercise I do – and have done most of my life. Nothing formal and nothing organised on a regular basis.

Do I put on weight?

Heck yes. We have bathroom scales at home but I only use them to weigh the suitcase before a flight. I stand on the scales and take a reading, then pick up the suitcase, get back on and take another reading. The difference is the weight of the suitcase. I mention this only to point out that I do not care how much I weigh.

What I care about is being able to fit into my trousers. Now that I'm older, I can afford nice clothes. I look after them. When I see things in my wardrobe that are too tight for me to wear I feel upset. So, I do something about it.

I reduce my food intake. My clothes become tight – I eat less.

There may be some of you who will struggle with this concept. We are not all the same. However, I would urge you to at least try this common-sense approach to staying in shape. Interested in knowing more? This is how it started for me.

Fasting

There was a TV programme in 2012 called Eat, Fast and Live Longer, presented by Dr Michael Mosley. The presenter was about my age, level of fitness and similar sedentary job. At the time of that programme airing, my daughter's wedding had just been announced, giving us six months' notice. I realised that I would have a short spell 'in the spotlight' and I had a really smart suit I had chosen to wear. But it was very tight. I had recorded the TV programme Eat, Fast and Live Longer, so I watched it again, I took note of what was being said and took it to heart.

I chose a plan whereby I would 'fast & feast' on alternate days. This is hard to believe from someone who would notoriously become "hangry" when deprived of food. I would eat food in the street or just having a walk out somewhere. I would be the person you would see at the supermarket checkout with empty wrappers, apologising to the shop assistant and scanning the eaten food wrappers through the till.

I believed that if I stopped eating I would collapse. So, I did not think I would last one day on this eating regime. I discovered I was safe though, because it was not a diet, it was a 'way of life'.

The regime allows you to eat only once on day one with reduced calories and then whatever you want on day two. Then repeat. I would have my first meal around 7pm one day and then have my normal three meals the next day. Over that six months until the wedding, I felt much better, slept better and – most importantly – got into that suit comfortably.

I mention that episode in my life because I learned a valuable lesson. We can easily get used to reducing our food intake. Believe me, if someone had brought this to me without the scientific study that was shown on TV, I would never have considered it to be achievable. The trick is to drink when you are hungry. Water, tea or coffee, without milk or sugar.

Now, when I feel my clothes getting tight, I reduce my intake. Either by a short spell of fasting and feasting or by drinking water when I am hungry.

What I've learned

By walking regularly, tidying the garden and doing jobs around the house, I remain in reasonable shape. By acting on the feedback coming from the waistband of my trousers, I can control my food intake.

There is no need to spend money on fancy diets or gym membership. Staying in control of our waistline is a mindset.

Speaking of mindset, I would like to drill down deeper on the subject mentioned in Chapter 1 – 'What we think about, we bring about' because this has a massive impact on our health.

We can take control of our own health

I said earlier that we are responsible for what happens in our lives and we create our future based on our thoughts and our feelings. What we think and how we feel creates our experiences – and determines whether or not we remain healthy.

Where's the evidence?

OK, now it gets tricky. We need to turn to the world of quantum physics to find an explanation and I am not a quantum scientist. The best reference I could point you to would be a film called, "What the bleep do we know?", which was made in 2004. I will provide here my own layman's explanation, which I hope helps to make it more clear and hopefully, not confuse you further.

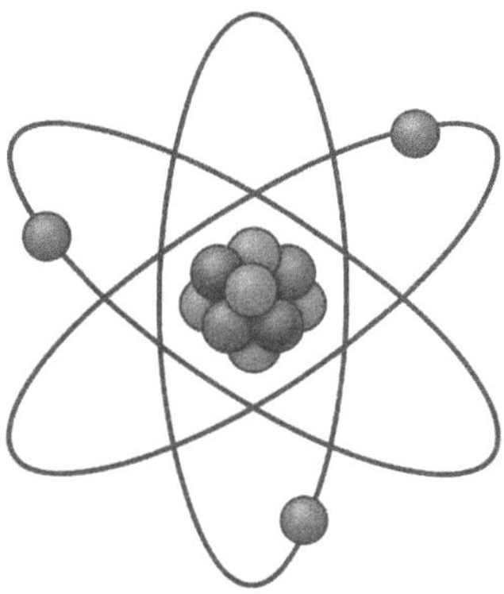

In one section of that film, they cover the basic structure of an atom. Imagine the simple picture you were shown at school with a nucleus in the centre, holding protons and neutrons and then electrons going around the nucleus, each in their own orbit (shown in this diagram on the left as the black circles forming ellipses round the outside of the inner circle). From that sketch you would imagine you could simply "take a look at" the electron, through complex scientific instruments. Well, you can, but not in the way you would imagine because this image of an atom is not how an atom is in the quantum world.

What the film shows is that the different elements of the atom are 'vibrating clouds of energy' moving around (shown in this diagram on the right as a cloud surrounding the nucleus). Then, when the scientist looks for, say, the electron, that 'vibrating energy cloud' collapses to form the solid object we think of as the electron. This is the effect that we have - ***when we set our intent*** on finding the electron, the energy field collapses and produces the matter we call the electron. Scientists call this the 'observer effect', which means the act of observing creates the matter. To me, this is at the heart of us humans creating matter all the time – and we have been doing this all of our lives.

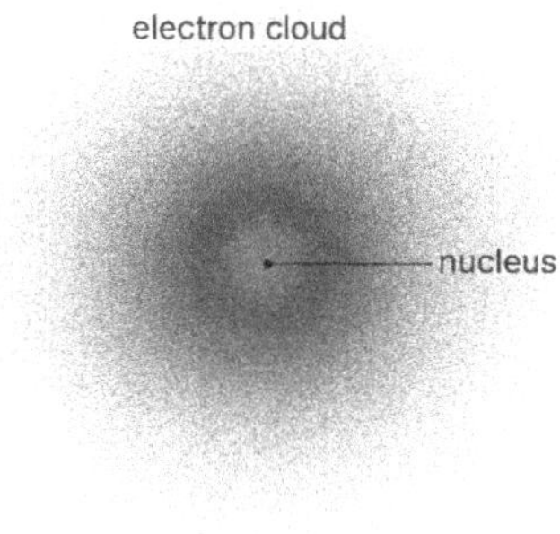

We decide we would like to see the electron, so the electron appears for us. We decide what we want to see in our lives and we ourselves are creating it that way.

It means that the 'vibrating energy clouds' are not a nucleus, electron or a proton but the potential to produce a nucleus, electron or a proton. This is key for me. The quantum world shows us that everything is purely ***potential*** – waiting for us to create what we want. And we are creating our worlds, second by second each day. We are setting our intent on how we believe our world is and then we are creating it for ourselves.

It means that every day, when we wake up, we create the world before us and the creative work is done by our subconscious mind. I love the fact that the word 'reactor' is an anagram of the word 'creator'. We think the world around us is being created and we are reacting to it. But the truth is, we are not reacting, we are creating. We need to change our mindset because we are not the reactor but the creator.

We humans are conditioned and, dare I say, lazy. So, the world we create each day is almost a replica of the last day. We do not believe we can create something majestical, so we go with the mundane and re-create yesterday. Not precisely yesterday – but we will get up from the same side of the bed, go to the bathroom the same way, do the same things we did yesterday in the bathroom, get dressed in similar clothes, eat a similar breakfast, listen to the same news station and read the same newspaper – and so on. Pretty much delivering the same experiences, more or less, as yesterday.

Even if we left ourselves a note by the bed telling us that tomorrow, things will be completely different and we will skip our way to the bathroom where we will be pampered by our beloved partner, massaged and helped on with our clothing then carried downstairs to our favourite breakfast already set out and all of our friends there to share breakfast with us. THAT WILL NOT HAPPEN. Because it is so far from what we consider reality that we simply could not ***believe*** it could happen. But it is only our belief that is holding back our aspirations.

Belief systems that shackle

Our belief systems, shaped by years of conditioning, can be powerful barriers to creating the life we desire. We've been taught to believe certain things about ourselves, the world, and our possibilities. These beliefs, often deeply ingrained, can limit our potential and perpetuate negative patterns.

But the truth is, you are not a victim of your circumstances. **You are the creator of your own reality**. Every day, through our thoughts, beliefs, and actions, we're shaping our future. The key to unlocking our full potential lies in understanding and transforming these belief systems.

Our subconscious mind, the hidden powerhouse of our psyche, holds a treasure trove of beliefs and emotions, many of which we're unaware. These beliefs, often formed in childhood, can continue to influence our thoughts and behaviours, even if we're no longer consciously aware of them.

Negative beliefs, rooted in fear, doubt, or limiting self-perceptions, can manifest as negativity in our lives. We might attract negative experiences, struggle with health issues, or find ourselves in toxic relationships. It's easy to blame external factors, but the truth lies within.

To create the life we desire, we must delve into our subconscious mind and address these negative beliefs. This can be done through various techniques, such as meditation, journaling, and therapy. By becoming aware of these limiting beliefs and challenging them, we can gradually reprogram our subconscious mind and create a more positive reality. There is a manifestation exercise in Chapter 1 that I truly hope you are practicing every day now and that you are seeing results.

Remember, change is possible. You're not trapped by your past. By understanding the power of your mind and taking proactive steps to shift your beliefs, you can break free from the chains of negativity and create the life you truly want. And this includes having **good health**. When we **don't** change our mind-set, we carry on creating the illnesses we have.

So, we have two influences, the first is what we believe and the second is what our subconscious is holding with regard to all our stored negativity from the past.

Consequently, most people create negativity in their lives and then they look around for who to blame.

Creating new cells

One thing that has always baffled me is the human body's constant renewal of cells. We are told that all of the cells in our body are replaced roughly every seven years. That's average, so some have a shorter life cycle. For example, new skin cells are produced in the lower regions of the epidermis and they are moved to the surface to replenish old skin cells **every four weeks**.

The scars we carry

Now, let's talk about a fascinating little mystery. When I was six, I was run over by a car whilst playing outside my house and ended up with a fractured skull and a nasty ankle injury. My skull healed beautifully, but I still have a prominent scar on my ankle, where it became stuck between the car tyre and the road surface. It's a constant reminder of that day, a physical marker of a painful experience.

But as we have covered above: skin cells are replaced every four weeks. So, why does my body continue to recreate this scar? Why hasn't it reverted to the original blueprint, creating new, unblemished skin?

It turns out, the answer lies in my mind. You see, I've conditioned my subconscious mind to believe that I have an old wound. It's like a well-worn groove in a record, playing the same tune over and over. Every day, as I create my reality, I'm subconsciously telling my body to recreate that scar.

This isn't just about physical wounds. We carry over old emotional and mental scars too. Maybe it's a grudge we've been holding onto for years, a fear that's been haunting us since childhood, or a limiting belief that's been holding us back. These wounds, just like the scar on my ankle, are often subconscious, deeply ingrained within us.

So, take a moment to reflect. What are you carrying over from your past? Are there any "old wounds", physical or mental, that are still affecting your life today? It might be a painful process to examine these wounds, but it's the first step towards healing.

Once we become aware of these old wounds, we can start to address them. We can challenge our limiting beliefs, let go of grudges, and cultivate a more positive mindset. It's like cleaning out a closet that's been filled with clutter for years. It might be messy at first, but the sense of relief and clarity you'll feel afterward is priceless.

We can choose – right now – which old memories we wish to retain and which of them we wish to let go.

You can even go so far as to 'alter' your memory if you wish. For example, if you had a troublesome family history, you could 're-invent' your family and tell yourself you were raised in a loving, supportive family. You could imagine you were the child of someone you know that is a loving parent. We cannot change the past but we can change the negative images we have of it. It's the letting go that frees us.

You need not be defined by your past. You have the power to create a new reality for yourself. So, let's start by shedding those old wounds and stepping into a brighter future.

Well, what can we do about it?

It is simply a matter of creating positivity and harmony in our subconscious to create a future for ourselves that is fulfilling, abundant, loving and joyous. To support this, I recommend you read, "You can heal your life", by Louise Hay.

When we think "I'm always unlucky", "Oh no, not again", "things like that always happen to me" and other similar thought patterns, we are creating the very negativity that we are bemoaning.

Alternatively, believing we are lucky, loved, living in richness and thoughts like that will create a world for us that reflects those beliefs.

Having positive thoughts or negative thoughts will create quite different experiences. What we believe is true will become true. Thoughts that dwell on negativity will make us unwell.

You will know positive happy people that draw positivity toward them. And we say, "misery loves company", showing that sad negative people draw similar folk toward themselves. And that those type of people usually have poor health and little wealth.

Every thought we choose to believe will create the corresponding life for us

The subconscious mind accepts what you choose to believe. What you believe about yourself will become true for you. And the unbelievably great news is – you have an unlimited amount of choice regarding what you can think.

First we have to accept that we should choose to believe that we are lucky, rather than unlucky – we are loved, rather than unloved – we are living in abundance, rather than living in poverty.

The point of power is always in the present moment

All the events you've experienced in your lifetime up to this moment have been created by your thoughts and beliefs you have held in the past. They were created by the thoughts and words you used yesterday, last week, last year, or any number of years ago depending on how old you are.

However, that is your past. It is over and done with. What is important in this moment is what you are choosing to think and believe and say right now. For these thoughts and words will create your future. Your point of power is in the present moment, and is forming the experience of tomorrow, next week, next month, next year and so on.

You might notice what thought you are thinking at this moment. Is it negative or positive? Do you want this thought to be creating your future? Just notice and be aware.

Believe it or not, we do choose our thoughts

We may habitually think the same thought over and over so that it does not seem like we're choosing the thought. But we did make the original choice. We can refuse to think certain thoughts.

Look how often you've refused to think a positive thought about yourself. Well, you can also refuse to think a negative thought about yourself.

It seems to me that everyone on this planet is suffering from self-dislike and guilt to one degree or another. The more self-dislike and guilt we have, the less our lives work. The less self-dislike and guilt we have, the better our lives work on all levels.

The innermost belief for most people is always, "I'm not good enough!"

We often add to that, "and I don't do enough" or "I don't deserve". Does this sound like you? Often saying or implying or feeling that you "are not good enough"? But for whom? And according to whose standards?

If this belief is very strong in you, then how can you possibly have created a loving, joyous, prosperous, healthy life? Somehow your main subconscious belief would always be contradicting it. Somehow, you would never quite get it together, for something would always be going wrong somewhere.

Resentment, criticism, guilt, and fear cause more problems than anything else

These four things cause the major problems in our bodies and in our lives. These feelings come from blaming others and not taking responsibility for our own experiences. You see, if we're all responsible for everything in our lives, then there is no one to blame. Whatever is happening "out there" is only a mirror of our own inner thinking. I am not condoning other people's poor behaviour, but it is OUR beliefs that attract people who will treat us that way.

If you find yourself saying "everyone always does such and such to me, criticises me, is never there for me, uses me like a doormat, abuses me," then this is your pattern. There is some thought in you that attracts people who exhibit this behaviour. When you no longer think that way, they will go elsewhere and do that to somebody else. You will no longer attract them.

Resentment that is long-held can eat away at the body and become the 'dis-ease' we call cancer. Criticism as a permanent habit can often lead to arthritis in the body. Guilt always looks for punishment, and punishment creates pain.

Forgiving and releasing resentment will dissolve even cancer

If we choose to believe we are helpless victims and that it's all hopeless, then our subconscious will support us in that belief, create that world for us, and we will just go down the drain. It is vital that we release these foolish, outmoded, negative ideas and beliefs that do not support us and nourish us.

To release the past, we must be willing to forgive

We need to choose to release the past and forgive everyone, ourselves included. We may not know how to forgive and we may not want to forgive, but the very fact that we say we are willing to forgive begins the healing process. It is imperative for our own healing that "we" release the past and forgive everyone.

"I forgive you for not being the way I wanted you to be. I forgive you and I set you free."

Loving and approving of ourselves

When people present with a problem, of poor health, lack of money, unfulfilling relationships or stifled creativity – there is only one thing to work on and that is LOVING THE SELF.

When we really love and accept and approve of ourselves exactly as we are, then everything in life works.

It's as if little miracles are everywhere. Our health improves, we attract more money, our relationships become more fulfilling, and we begin to express ourselves in creatively fulfilling ways. All this seems to happen without our even trying.

Loving and approving of yourself, creating a space of safety, trusting and deserving and accepting, will create organisation in your mind, create more loving relationships in your life, attract a new job and a new and better place to live and, even enable your body weight to normalise. People who love themselves and their bodies neither abuse themselves nor others. So, consider looking here first if you are carrying excess weight.

Self-approval and self-acceptance 'in the now' are the main keys to positive changes in every area of our lives.

Loving the self begins with never ever criticising ourselves for anything. Criticism locks us into the very pattern we are trying to change. Understanding and being gentle with ourselves helps us to move out of it. You have been criticising yourself for years and it hasn't worked. Try approving of yourself and see what happens.

What else impacts our physical wellbeing?

Having explained how our subconscious mind is the major influence on our health, it seems fair to at least look at other things that could also play minor roles. Only in the sense that if we are struggling with where we live, for example, that in itself will impact how we feel about ourselves and the messages we pass to our subconscious.

Our environment can have an impact on our physical wellbeing. This includes factors such as air, water, and food. If you find yourself with issues in these areas then please start making steps now to improve or move.

The things we do every day will affect how we feel and think about ourselves. Included in that is our diet. A healthy diet includes plenty of fruits, vegetables, whole grains, and lean protein.

Regular physical activity (walking, gardening, housework, etc) can improve our mood and energy levels.

Smoking will set our expectation that we are at risk from cancer. That in itself will make us susceptible because of our internal dialogue with our subconscious and then by extension, our outcomes will be based on those intentions.

Alcohol is similar to smoking in that we may set the intention that it's harmful because of what we've been told to believe. I continue to drink alcohol every day by having a glass of lager with dinner. I don't believe this is in any way detrimental to my health – and therefore it will not be. I believe the lager is helping to 'flush' my liver and kidneys. Despite statistics that will tell me otherwise, I **believe** this to be the case in **my** body. That belief is carried through my cells and, in truth, I don't know how they do their magic but they carry on functioning and treating lager as harmless.

We may already have certain health conditions and they will affect how we feel about ourselves. However, we can halt the decline.

Important Note: Please continue to follow any advice you are receiving from your health care providers. The information I am providing on how the subconscious mind is creating the life we lead is to help you make changes to your mind-set. 'What we think about, we bring about' also means that if we believe our doctor's advice is helping us, then it will.

So, current conditions should follow current recommendations. In addition to those recommendations, there are additional things you can do to halt the worsening of conditions, help prevent new illness and potentially heal yourself.

What we can do to improve our physical wellbeing

Our bodies are conditioned almost exactly the same way as they were 700,000 years ago. The evolution of our human bodies has taken hundreds of thousands of years. The ability to produce food has massively increased in pace just over the 70 years I've been on the planet. Which means our bodies could not have kept pace with the changes in how we live now.

Back when we lived in caves, we might have some success at hunting and bring the quarry home, where we would prepare it and eat it. If we were lucky, it might last more than one day. Then we would set off hunting again. But during this time there would be nothing to eat. So, we would have enforced 'fasting & feasting' – lean periods followed by times of plenty. Exactly like the regime

I covered earlier in this chapter, when explaining my own experiences after watching Dr Michael Mosley on TV.

Fast forward to now and the world of providing food has changed beyond recognition. But our bodies still process food as if we were cave dwellers.

We have freezers, refrigerators, cupboards to store foods, fast food outlets, local convenience stores – and so on. Some of our food, like rice and pasta can be stored for a very long time. It's fair to say, we are bombarded with food now compared to our ancestors living in caves.

Our evolution allowed our digestive systems to develop and adapt to our environment. We ate what we killed or harvested. And what was around us was "good for us" because it matched how our bodies processed the food. Now, at this level of our evolution, there is a mismatch.

As we became more 'developed' as humans, we settled on new ways to make sure we found and produced food more quickly and found ways to store it more easily. After hundreds of thousands of years, we have become very adept at food production. But what we eat now is not all nutritious or beneficial for us, given that we are still pretty much built like our ancient ancestors.

A healthy diet for a healthy you

So, you're wondering what you can eat to keep yourself feeling great? Well, the good news is there's a whole world of delicious and nutritious options out there.

Let's start with some powerhouses: fish, broccoli, and other cruciferous vegetables. These are packed with vitamins, minerals, and antioxidants that can help protect your cells from damage. Beets are a great source of fibre and nitrates, which can improve blood flow and lower blood pressure. Spinach and other leafy green vegetables are full of iron, calcium, and vitamin K. Kale, on the other hand, is a superfood that's packed with nutrients and can help boost your immune system.

For a healthy dose of protein and fibre, try peanut butter and almonds. And if you're craving something sweet, don't worry, you can still indulge in a bit of chocolate (in moderation, of course). It's a great source of antioxidants and can even boost your mood.

If you're looking for a balanced and nutritious meal, consider the Mediterranean diet. This diet is rich in fruits, vegetables, whole grains, legumes, and healthy fats. It's been linked to a lower risk of heart disease, stroke, and type 2 diabetes.

And let's not forget about quinoa and pickled vegetables. Quinoa is a complete protein that's also high in fibre and nutrients. Pickled vegetables are a great way to add flavour and crunch to your meals while also getting a dose of probiotics.

So, there you have it! A variety of delicious and nutritious foods that can help you stay healthy and feel your best. Remember, variety is key, so don't be afraid to experiment and find what works best for you.

What about exercise?

Now, I'm not one for hitting the gym or following strict workout routines. I'm more of a "keep moving" kind of person. But I understand that for many, exercise is a recreational activity they enjoy. And let me tell you, it's not just good for your body, it's a fantastic way to boost your mood and create positive vibes. In fact, as you have seen earlier in this chapter, I believe that creating a positive mindset is the number one thing you can do to improve your life.

Exercise is like a magic potion for your mind. It helps to reduce stress, improve your memory, and even boost your creativity. When you're feeling good physically, it's easier to feel good mentally. And that positive mindset will have a positive ripple effect on your entire life.

So, whether you're into dancing, swimming, hiking, or simply taking a brisk walk, find something you enjoy and make it a regular part of your routine. Remember, it's not about being perfect; it's about finding what works for you and sticking with it.

And here's a little secret: exercise can be a great way to meet new people and make friends. Join a local sports team, take a dance class, or even just start a walking group with your neighbours.

Swimming offers a fantastic cardiovascular workout, improving your heart health and endurance.

Cycling is a great activity that strengthens your legs, core, and cardiovascular system.

Yoga is a journey of mind-body connection. Yoga not only improves your flexibility and balance, but it also strengthens your core and promotes relaxation.

Tai chi calls for gentle movements that flow together like a calming wave. That's the beauty of tai chi, an ancient Chinese practice that's perfect for us more mature people.

Walking is my chosen exercise. I find it therapeutic being in nature and it provides the ‘space’ we all need to halt our busy lives and take time out to think.

The 8 minute workout

If I were to recommend anything in addition to the things I've stated above that work for me (walking, gardening, beekeeping and maintenance in the home) I would be drawn to **isometric exercise** because of how much time they take up and the fact that they need no equipment to practice.

You can go for a cardio-boosting run, add a bit of yoga for flexibility and throw in some weight training to keep your muscles strong if you're really good: we all know what we ought to be doing every week to stay healthy in midlife. But now research suggests that static isometric exercises, which involve using your muscles to hold your body still in certain positions, are even more effective at reducing your blood pressure and therefore your risk of heart attacks, strokes and vascular dementia.

In a review of 270 clinical trials involving 15,827 participants that was published in the British Medical Journal this year, Dr Jamie O'Driscoll, a researcher in cardiovascular physiology at Canterbury Christ Church University, describes how isometric moves, such as a plank or a wall sit, could be helpful not only for the 14 million people in the UK who already have hypertension but **everyone of middle-age and older**.

"When people think about resistance exercise they assume it involves a lot of dynamic movement such as repetitive weightlifting or lunges and squats," O'Driscoll says.

"Isometric exercise is overlooked but is something we should all be adding to the mix."

Rather than performing endless repetitions with increasingly heavy weights, eight minutes of isometric exercises — such as planks, wall sits and squat holds — three times a week could bring benefits for heart health while boosting balance, posture and muscular endurance.

O'Driscoll's research compared the effects of aerobic cardio exercise, such as running and cycling; repetitions of dynamic movements, such as press-ups and squats; HIIT training, which involves intense effort followed by periods of recovery, and isometric workouts on blood pressure.

Results showed that all exercise was helpful in reducing hypertension, but that static exercise was the most effective. "When you work a muscle isometrically by holding it under tension with no movement, blood vessels compress," O'Driscoll says. "When you release the hold there is a sudden increase in blood flow as the blood vessels dilate again, which is an effect you don't get in the same way with other forms of exercise."

His paper is the latest to outline the importance of isometric training for heart health. Three years ago, isometric exercise was added to the European Society of Cardiology guidelines on sports cardiology and exercise in patients with cardiovascular disease for the first time, and in other published studies O'Driscoll and his colleagues have shown that static exercise reduces inflammation, improves performance of the heart and reduces the acceleration of cardiovascular disease.

But benefits extend beyond the cardiovascular. "What these exercises do very well is improve muscle endurance, or the capacity of muscles to sustain effort," Dalton Wong, the founder of TwentyTwo Training, says. "This is very important when it comes to maintaining good posture and stability."

Adding isometric exercises to your routine will also make your muscles stronger. "The real beauty of static training is that it requires little or no equipment — you can do it using your own body weight — and it is supremely time efficient," Wong says. "I like to do my isometric moves at the end of a workout to maximise the gains in muscle endurance. But you can get great health gains from doing just a few minutes on a regular basis." He suggests choosing **any four** of the isometric exercises below to hold for two minutes each — a total of **eight minutes a workout** — with two minutes' rest in between.

"We have just completed a study on people in their eighties, who were able to do an isometric routine quite easily," O'Driscoll adds. "If you need to stop, stand up, or kneel, momentarily to ease the load, then return to the position to finish the two-minute bout. The crucial thing is to do it a few times a week."

Dalton Wong's isometric routine

Choose four exercises to hold for two minutes each

Plank

Lie face down with your elbows on the ground. Raise your body so your elbows are at 90 degrees and your weight is distributed over your forearms and feet. Keep your back in line with your head and feet, looking down towards your hands and engage your core muscles to hold for two minutes. You can also try what is called a high plank — with straight arms supported by your hands, as if doing press-ups — but this can be challenging if you have weak wrists.

Bear plank

Start on your hands and knees with your weight evenly distributed. Engage your glutes (bottom) and core to lift your knees slightly off the ground. Keep your eyes on the floor and lower your back so it's slightly rounded but not arched. Hold this position for two minutes, lowering your knees momentarily if it is too tough.

V-sit

Start by lying on the floor. Simultaneously raise your upper and lower body to form a V position, with your core engaged, knees slightly bent, feet just off the ground and arms straight out in front of you. Hold for two minutes. If you need to, place your hands on the floor for support.

Squat

Stand upright, with your back straight and feet wider than hip width apart (an even wider squat will place less stress on your knees). Bend from the hips, keeping your weight over your heels and lowering your bottom until your thighs are parallel to the ground, or as low as is manageable. Hold for two minutes.

Standing scaption raises

Stand with your knees slightly bent, holding a dumbbell in each hand at your sides, with your thumbs at the highest point. Keeping your arms straight, raise the weights to shoulder height in front of you in a wide V, so that you feel a stretch across the

shoulders. Squeeze your shoulder blades together and engage the core muscles to hold for two minutes.

Wall sit

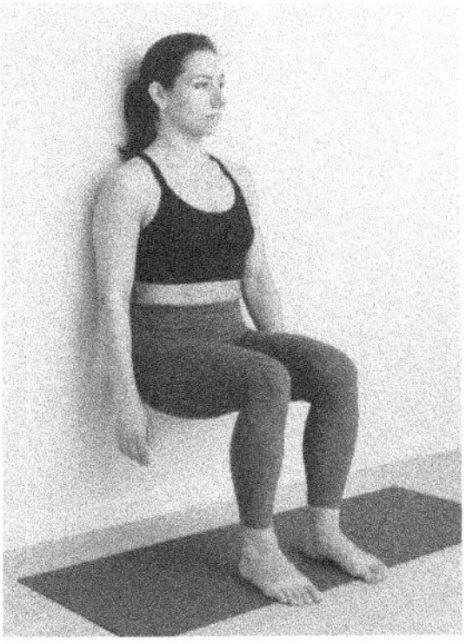

Stand with your back against a wall and feet shoulder width apart. Slowly slide your back down the wall, inching your feet forwards, until your thighs are parallel to the ground or at an angle that feels comfortable to hold (it's better to start in a moderate position). Make sure your knees are above your ankles and keep your back flat on the wall. Hold this position for two minutes.

Bridge

Lie on your back with your hands by your sides, knees bent and feet flat on the floor. Tighten your glutes, engage your core and lift your hips towards the ceiling until you have a straight line from your shoulders to your knees. Hold this position for two minutes.

What else can I be doing?

One of my biggest regrets is that I discovered meditation very late in life. Really only two or three years ago.

I believe meditation plays a big part in our wellbeing, both regarding health and mental health. I spend at least thirty minutes each morning in meditation. It's not always the same routine. We all would benefit from finding that stillness of the mind. Cutting out that inner 'voice' that criticises and nags us.

There are many ways to meditate; find what works for you.

I started by finding guided meditations on YouTube and listening to them through headphones. Now I just sit silently and focus on my breathing. There are seven main chakras in the body according to Hindu and Buddhist traditions. I think of each of them in turn, starting at the lowest and going up. The chakras are in a straight vertical line and their locations in the body are explained here.

The Seven Chakras: Energy centres of the body

Actually, there are many more than seven energy centres in the body. However, in general, most people when speaking of chakras are referring to the seven main ones. For example, we have minor energy centres in the palms of our hands.

Chakras are considered to be shaped like cones. They have the circular shape of the base of the cone under the skin and the pointed tip of the cone pointing in to the body.

There are seven **main** chakras, each associated with a specific colour, body part, and function. Each of these chakras has a "mate" with which they work in tandem. Their matching mate is on the back of the body, aligned with the chakra at the front. In the case of the root chakra, at the base of the spine, its mate is the crown chakra, at the top of the head. I often 'see' the root chakra with a silver twine stretched tight between its tip and the tip of the crown chakra. Then, I 'see' the other five chakras with the same connection between front and back – in pairs in line with the spine.

1. **Root Chakra**: Located at the base of the spine, this chakra is associated with grounding and survival. It governs our sense of security, stability, and connection to the physical world.

2. **Sacral Chakra**: Situated below the navel, this chakra is linked to creativity, passion, and pleasure. It governs our sexuality, emotions, and ability to enjoy life.

3. **Solar Plexus Chakra**: Located in the solar plexus, just below the lowest point of breastbone or sternum, this chakra is associated with self-esteem, confidence, and personal power. It governs our sense of self-worth and ability to achieve our goals.

4. **Heart Chakra**: Found in the centre of the chest, this chakra is linked to love, compassion, and forgiveness. It governs our ability to connect with others, give and receive love, and experience joy.

5. **Throat Chakra**: Located in the throat, this chakra is associated with communication, self-expression, and truth. It governs our ability to speak our minds, express our creativity, and connect with others on a deeper level.

6. **Third Eye Chakra**: Situated between the eyebrows, this chakra is linked to intuition, wisdom, and inner vision. It governs our ability to perceive the world beyond the physical senses and tap into our inner knowing.

7. Crown Chakra: Located at the crown of the head, this chakra is associated with spirituality, enlightenment, and connection to a higher power. It governs our sense of connection to the universe and our ability to access our full potential.

When our chakras are balanced, we feel energised, centred, and fulfilled. However, when they become blocked or imbalanced, we may experience physical, emotional, or mental challenges. Practices like meditation, yoga, and energy healing can help to balance the chakras and promote overall well-being.

Finding Your Inner Peace: A Meditation Guide

Meditation is a powerful tool for cultivating inner peace and well-being. It's a practice that involves focusing the mind on a single point, such as the breath or a mantra. While it may seem simple, it can be surprisingly challenging, especially for beginners.

What I find helpful is the audible exhale. I take a deep breath, hold for three seconds and then exhale with a little bit of force – just enough so that I can hear the exhale. In addition, I roll my eyes under my eyelids as if I'm looking at my eyebrows. These two actions – the sound of my breath leaving and my eyes being pointed up, act like barriers to my mind wandering in with distracting thoughts.

That is the common obstacle to meditation – the constant stream of thoughts that can bombard the mind. Our ego-centric mind constantly wants our attention. When this happens, it's helpful to gently bring your attention back to your chosen focus. A technique I find particularly effective is to start at the root chakra and work my way up to the crown chakra, taking deep breaths at each point. This helps to ground me and calm my mind. Before I knew anything about chakras (or even meditation), I used to start at my feet then work up to my knees, thighs, bottom and so on, up to my head. You can choose whichever way you wish, there is no right or wrong.

After practice, you will be able to switch off your mind quite quickly and easily. Then you might decide to concentrate on your breathing and go straight to one part of your body (I choose just below my navel) and just stay in that quiet space.

If you find yourself getting distracted by thoughts from your day, don't be discouraged. Simply acknowledge the thought and gently return your focus to your breath or mantra. With practice, you'll become better at letting go of distractions and finding a sense of inner peace. If you find yourself falling asleep, don't be discouraged. It happens and it simply means your body needed the rest. If you can, just start your 'routine' of meditation again.

Once you've mastered the art of quieting the mind, you'll be able to experience the profound benefits of meditation. These include reduced stress, improved focus, and increased emotional well-being.

I'm sure everyone has their own unique experience during meditation. In my case, I can feel the stages as I 'descend' into stillness. The first thing I notice is that the "voice in my head" is less prevalent. Eventually, I move to a condition where I can't feel my limbs. I can sense they are there and I can move them if I wish. As I go deeper, I can feel less of my body and yet, as with the limbs, I know everything is in order. That is the space I am aiming for. It's peaceful. No nagging about what my mind thinks I 'should' be doing.

One of the most powerful aspects of meditation is its ability to help you cultivate a sense of detachment from negative thoughts and emotions. When you're able to observe your thoughts without judgment, you're less likely to be swept away by them.

This can be incredibly helpful in dealing with life's challenges. When I am feeling stressed or upset, I can remind myself of the peace I have experienced earlier in the day, during meditation. This can help me let go of negative thoughts and emotions and respond to situations with greater calm and clarity.

Meditation takes time and practice to develop the skills necessary to quiet the mind. But the rewards are well worth the effort. So, I encourage you to give it a try. You might be surprised at how quickly you can start to experience the benefits. And, there are lots of guided meditations on YouTube, where you simply follow instruction.

Five successful people who meditate

There are estimates that as many as 500 million people on the planet meditate. Not everyone declares it openly. It is surprising how many well-known, public figures use meditation in their daily lives. Here are just five of them, to give you an idea of the cross-section of the population and their reasons for meditating.

Oprah Winfrey: This iconic talk show host and media mogul has been open about her meditation practice. She often talks about how meditation has helped her find inner peace, reduce stress, and gain clarity.

Arianna Huffington: The founder of the Huffington Post and Thrive Global is a vocal advocate for meditation. She believes that meditation is essential for our mental and physical health, and she has even written books on the subject.

Paul McCartney: Songwriter for The Beatles has long been a frequent meditator. McCartney started meditating in the 60s and still does so today. “I think it’s always very good to get a sort of still moment in your day. Whenever I have a chance in a busy schedule, I’ll do it, if I’m not rushing out the door with some crazy stuff to do. But yeah, I always like to take a moment and just meditate.”

Arnold Schwarzenegger: The former bodybuilder and actor has incorporated meditation into his daily routine. He believes that meditation has helped him stay focused, reduced stress and achieve his goals.

Ray Dalio: The billionaire hedge fund manager is a proponent of meditation. He believes that meditation has helped him make better decisions and improve his relationships.

Summary

Growing up, enforced fasting was a regular occurrence, and walking everywhere was my primary mode of transportation. Looking back, I can see how these experiences shaped my relationship with health.

Those early days taught me the value of resourcefulness and adaptability. And when I had to walk miles to get anywhere, I developed a level of physical endurance that has served me well throughout my life.

But perhaps the most valuable lesson I learned was the power of the mind. Despite the hardships I faced, I always maintained a sense of optimism and resilience. I **believed** that I could overcome any challenge, and that **belief** has been a driving force in my life. When you believe in yourself, you're more likely to take care of yourself, to set goals, and to persevere through difficulties.

It’s what we believe that matters

At the quantum level, particles exist in a state of superposition, meaning they can be in multiple states simultaneously until observed. This suggests that the universe is constantly fluctuating and is pure **potential**.

Our beliefs, our intentions, act as filters, selecting specific outcomes from this quantum soup. They shape the reality we experience. It's like tuning a radio to a specific frequency; our beliefs determine the channel we receive.

The universe is a mirror reflecting our inner world. By changing our beliefs, we can change our reality. It's a journey of self-discovery and self-improvement.

Creating a healthier you

Exercise is a no-brainer. Even a short walk can do wonders for your physical and mental health. Eating is all about balance. You don't have to become a health nut overnight but try to fill your plate with lots of fruits, vegetables, and whole grains.

Meditation might sound a bit woo-woo, but it's a powerful tool for improving your well-being. It helps to calm your mind, reduce stress, and boost your mood. And when you feel good mentally, it's easier to make healthy choices physically.

But perhaps **the most important factor is our mindset**. Believe it or not, our thoughts and beliefs can have a profound impact on our health. When we believe that we can create a happy and healthy life, we're more likely to take the necessary steps to make it happen.

How we influence our bodies negatively

Our bodies are constantly responding to our beliefs. The way we think and feel shapes our well-being, and when we shift our beliefs, we open the door to healing and transformation. This isn't something reserved for a select few – it's possible for all of us when we understand how it works.

Our thoughts create our world, and those thoughts come from the beliefs we've picked up over time. If we want to change our reality, we have to start from within. Growth doesn't happen overnight – it's a gradual process, like climbing a staircase one step at a time. Big, sudden changes can feel overwhelming, but small, steady shifts make lasting transformation possible.

Looking to outside things – whether it's material success or other people – to "fix" us won't work. Real change starts inside because the world around us reflects what's happening in our minds and hearts. We have the power to shape our lives in ways that bring us more joy, peace, and fulfilment. When we listen to our true desires and passions, we start creating the life we were meant to live.

How we can influence our bodies positively

The first step to healing is forgiveness – both of your body and yourself. Instead of criticising your body, try thanking it for showing you where your inner struggles are. Every ache or imbalance is just a message, helping you understand what needs to change. Also, forgive yourself for believing things that weren't true or for making choices based on misinformation. These two simple acts – forgiving your body and yourself – set the stage for real healing.

Forgiveness brings peace of mind, and when your mind is at peace, your body can begin to heal. Our natural state is love, and it's up to us to align with that energy. When we hold onto anger, fear, or resentment – whether toward ourselves, others, or even our own bodies – we create stress that blocks healing. Letting go of judgment makes room for balance, well-being, and inner calm.

Please be careful. If you're taking medication, keep following your doctor's advice, but also try adding forgiveness practices to your daily routine. As your mindset shifts, you might find that your body starts feeling better too. If you ever decide to reduce medications, do it slowly and with awareness – your beliefs play a big role in how your body responds.

Healing isn't just about physical changes; it's about transforming the way you think and feel. By filling your mind with peace and love, you open the door to a healthier, happier life. You have the power to create the change you want – one small step at a time.

Further reading

A recommended read on this subject is **"Perfect Health"** by Deepak Chopra. He speaks of our different body types and how we help ourselves through specific diets and exercise, aimed at our body type.

Deepak Chopra also provides his view on how our subconscious creates our lives – including our illnesses. He goes deeply into what he calls, "quantum healing" and he explains how meditation can change the physical human body far easier than any drug, diet or exercise.

And of course, it's worth reading **"You can heal your life"** by Louise Hay. I have used some of her ideas in this chapter and you will get much better guidance directly from the lady herself.

We all know that a strong foundation is built on both physical and mental wellbeing. You've laid the groundwork for the former. Now, prepare to unlock the power of the latter... Your mind awaits, in the next chapter....

Chapter 3 – Mental wellbeing

"We will grieve not but rather find strength in what remains behind."

William Wordsworth - "Intimations of Immortality"

The topics chosen for this book cover a wide range of support for you and I aged from 60 onwards. This subject scores highly in terms of importance because of the impact of mental wellbeing on your overall welfare. And this is also very important as you mature. When we are unhappy within ourselves, we are usually also unhappy with those people around us and unhappy with our lives in general.

It would be a little short-sighted if we all look after ourselves with regarding health and wealth, yet we fail ourselves regarding mental welfare. We might find ourselves healthy and rich but unable to leave the house.

Subjects in this chapter:

- Mental health of an ageing population
- Stress – the good, the bad and the ugly
- Checking in on your own stress levels
- My own experience of stress
- What we can do ward off mental challenges

What is Mental Wellbeing?

Have you ever noticed how everything seems manageable when you're in a good mood?

Or how a problem doesn't seem so serious after you've woken up from a good rest?

Ever noticed how a phone call to a friend makes you feel so much better?

Mental wellbeing is more than just the absence of mental illness. It's a state of positive mental health that allows us to cope with life's challenges, reach our full potential, and contribute to our communities. It's about feeling good, thinking clearly, and connecting with others meaningfully.

When you are in a good mental state, you are better equipped to handle stress, solve problems, and build strong relationships. You are more likely to make healthy choices, pursue your passions, and find joy in life. Conversely, poor mental health can lead to feelings of sadness, anxiety, and hopelessness, affecting your overall quality of life.

The effects of our mental health are experienced in every aspect of our lives. Our moods, physical health, and social connections help us cope better with adversity and unexpected hurdles.

By taking care of our mental health, we can improve our overall quality of life and live more fulfilling lives. With the right tools and support, we can all achieve a state of optimal mental wellbeing.

Mental disorder

Mental health conditions among older people are often underrecognised and undertreated because their conditions are not reported. Any figures provided in research are likely to be under-estimates due to the fact that we 'mature people' do not like to make a fuss about anything, do we?

This is partly our “just get on with things” attitude to life but also because of the stigma of declaring oneself to be struggling mentally. A stigma that people of any age would have but it’s far more humiliating for the elderly to be suspected of ‘losing their marbles’.

Let me get you started here with some key facts.

- By 2030, one in six people in the world will be aged 60 years or over.
- Loneliness and social isolation are key risk factors for mental health conditions in later life.
- One in six older adults experience abuse, often by their own carers.
- Approximately 14% of adults aged 60 and over live with a mental disorder.

Ageing across the globe

The world’s population is ageing fast. In 2020, 1 billion people in the world were aged 60 years or over. That figure will rise to 1.4 billion by 2030, representing one in six people globally. By 2050, the number of people aged 60 years and over will have doubled to reach 2.1 billion. The number of persons aged 80 years or older is expected to triple between 2020 and 2050 to reach 426 million.

Older adults contribute to society as family and community members, and many are volunteers and workers. While most have good health, many are at risk of developing mental health conditions such as depression and anxiety disorders. Many may also experience reduced mobility, chronic pain, frailty, dementia, or other health problems, for which they require some form of long-term care. As people age, they are more likely to experience several conditions at the same time.

Prevalence

I would just like to pick up on that last bullet point above, were it says around 14% of people over 60 are living with a mental disorder. According to the Global Health Estimates (GHE) 2019, these conditions account for 10.6% of the total disability (in disability adjusted life years) among older adults. The most common mental health conditions for older adults are depression and anxiety. GHE 2019 shows that globally, around a quarter of deaths from suicide (27.2%) are among people aged 60 or over.

Risk factors

At older ages, mental health is shaped not only by physical and social environments but also by the cumulative impacts of earlier life experiences and specific stressors related to ageing. Exposure to adversity, and a decline in functional ability can result in psychological distress.

Older adults are more likely to experience adverse events such as bereavement, or a drop in income or a reduced sense of purpose with retirement. Despite their many contributions to society, many older adults are subject to ageism, which can seriously affect their mental health.

Social isolation and loneliness, which affect about a quarter of us older people, are key risk factors for mental health conditions in later life. So too is abuse of older people, which includes any kind of physical, verbal, psychological, sexual or financial abuse, as well as neglect. Abuse of older adults has serious consequences and can lead to depression and anxiety.

Many older people are carers of spouses with chronic health conditions, such as dementia. The responsibilities of such care can be overwhelming and can affect the carer's mental health. Later we will discuss my personal story and how my mental health was jeopardised in this regard and explain what happened when I was full-time (and only) carer for my wife. When I look back now, I can see that I was in a deep hole of depression and I felt like our health service had washed it's hands of me.

Some older adults are at greater risk of depression and anxiety, because of dire living conditions, poor physical health, or lack of access to quality support and services. This includes older adults living in humanitarian settings and those living with chronic illnesses (such as heart disease, cancer, or stroke), neurological conditions (such as dementia), or substance abuse problems.

Then there's the factor of our internal narrative that we have built up over decades, with regard to the negative thoughts and feelings we have suppressed. We've covered 'what we think about, we bring about' in the last chapter and it plays incredibly strongly into our mental health in later life.

If we reach old age with the belief that it will result in poverty, loneliness, ill-health, and so on – then it invariably will.

Whereas, when you believe what I am putting forward in this book, that you are creating your own life from your subconscious mind, then one of the first things you have to do is work on your mindset.

Stress

When we think of stress, we often think of it as a bad thing. But did you know that stress can actually be beneficial in some situations? That's right, stress can sometimes be good for us. It can help us to perform better, to stay motivated, and to learn and grow.

So, before we do a deep dive into the negative effects of stress, it's worth just thinking about the place of stress in our evolution and right up to modern day.

Stress can help us to learn and to grow as individuals. When we are challenged, we are forced to adapt and to learn new things. This can make us stronger and more resilient.

Of course, too much stress can be harmful. But if we can learn to manage our stress effectively, it can actually be a good thing. It is core to us as humans. When we lived in caves over 700,000 years ago, we were in survival mode and needed the hormones released by stress to get through each day. Stress helped us get up to go out and hunt for food. It helped us evade predators. It helped us provide for our offspring.

Now, in the 21st century, we do not switch those hormones off – and that is what is stressful. Imagine our caveman ancestor going out hunting. They would need to be careful that the rustle in the bushes they hear is their lunch, rather than the other way around. If they discovered that they were being viewed by the predator as their next meal, these stress hormones would be accelerated through the body and help our ancestor escape. Then they would find shelter and sanctuary while the danger receded. So, the hormones would spike and then reduce. Whereas these days, we continue to 'chew over' the thing that has caused us stress, going over it again and again, inducing more stress.

You could probably cite examples of this but let me share one of my own. A colleague in the workplace comes in one morning and is very much 'out of sorts'. They are incredibly quick to let you know what is troubling them. Some other driver has done something that the colleague has seen to be a personal affront. They go over this many times as they encounter other colleagues for the first time that day and they are re-creating the feeling, plus all the stress hormones. They carry this 'stone in their shoe' all day and it creates stress in them and tension in their colleagues.

For another mental picture, please imagine a small zebra crossing the plains in the Serengeti when a lion starts a chase. Huge amounts of adrenaline and cortisol immediately kick in and prepare the zebra for flight. The high levels are only suitable for a short time – but usually that is all that is needed. When the zebra can see there is no more danger, the adrenaline and cortisol production reduces and the massive spike is over. You will see the zebra simply go back to grazing as if nothing had happened. This is how our ancestors were. But modern homo sapiens keep those chemicals pumping.

The zebra is living 'in the now'. Whereas the human of today will be living in the past in his or her head by going through the experience repeatedly in their head and continue the flow of negative chemicals. This then becomes a huge 'cost' to our systems. Adrenaline makes the heart beat faster and raises your blood pressure, whilst cortisol slows nonessential functions, suppresses the digestive system, the reproductive system and growth processes. Then there are messages sent to the brain that control mood, motivation and fear.

This puts you at higher risk of many health problems, including:

- Anxiety
- Depression
- Digestive problems
- Headaches
- Muscle tension and pain
- Heart disease, heart attack, high blood pressure and stroke
- Sleep problems
- Weight gain
- Problems with memory and focus

This is another example of the 'reptile brain' we all possess being truly awesome in helping us to evolve and now it is hindering our progress and stoking our stress.

Elder stress

Stress in an aged population, also known as elder stress, encompasses the specific challenges and vulnerabilities older adults face when dealing with stressful situations. It's important to understand that stress for older adults differs from stress in younger individuals in several key ways:

Sources of Stress:

Health concerns: Chronic illnesses, declining physical abilities, and the threat of cognitive decline are major sources of stress for older adults.

Financial worries: Fixed incomes, rising healthcare costs, and potential dependence on others can create significant financial stress.

Social isolation: Loss of spouse, friends, or social connections can lead to loneliness and isolation, increasing stress levels.

Changes in living arrangements: Moving to assisted living facilities, experiencing relocation, or downsizing can be stressful and disruptive.

Loss of independence: Dependence on others for daily activities can be a major source of frustration and stress for older adults.

Fear of the future: Uncertainty about the future, including long-term care needs and financial security, can be a significant stressor.

Vulnerability to Stress:

Physiological changes: Age-related decline in physical and cognitive functioning can make older adults more susceptible to the negative effects of stress.

Reduced coping mechanisms: Older adults may have fewer resources and coping mechanisms to deal with stress compared to younger individuals.

Social stigma: Societal stereotypes about ageing can make it difficult for older adults to seek help for stress or mental health issues.

Impact of Stress:

Physical health: Chronic stress can exacerbate existing health conditions, increase the risk of heart disease, stroke, and other chronic illnesses.

Mental health: Stress can contribute to anxiety, depression, and cognitive decline in older adults.

Quality of life: Stress can negatively impact daily functioning, social relationships, and overall well-being.

By understanding the unique nature of stress in an aged population, we can better support ourselves (and others we know in our age range and approaching our age range) in managing stress levels and promoting overall well-being.

Stress is not an inevitable part of ageing, and proactive measures will help us all live healthier and happier lives.

Effects of stress on our physical health

As we have seen, stress has an effect on our health. So, let's dive a little deeper into that now by examining the thoughts of David R. Hawkins in "Letting Go".

Stress is our response to a perceived threat and the stimulus of that threat can be internal or external. It can be physical, mental or emotional. Research into the body's physical response to stress shows that when our body responds to a stressful stimulus, the body goes first through an alarm reaction, then secondly a stage of resistance, and if the stimulus continues, it may result in the third stage of exhaustion.

The first stage, the alarm, causes hormones to be released in our brain to stimulate our nervous system. This causes adrenaline to be sent out to prepare us for fight or flight.

There are many people, by the time they get to age 60, who have learned to live off the adrenaline high because of the constant challenges in their lives. The threat to survival keeps the adrenaline flowing. They get addicted to the excitement and abnormal stimulation. They get used to the semi euphoria because of the high levels of cortisol.

In the second stage, our body tries to correct itself. Hormonal changes shift our metabolism and alter the balance of minerals, often including sodium, which causes water retention. We may find that we get swollen ankles. We might also feel a let-down due to a decrease in the level of cortisol in our body. Cortisol also has an anaesthetic effect. So, during the let-down, we start complaining of aches and pains that weren't experienced before. I have experienced this after very busy periods of work, followed by a vacation – and then I've fallen sick whilst on holiday.

During the third stage we are exhausted, and if we continue to stress, our body's coping mechanisms will fail. Our body's defences fight against the effects of stress, blocking our immune system. Because it has now been going on for so long, our body's organs start to show changes due to the stress hormones we've been producing. Our 'fuel tanks' will be running on empty, which will lead to disease and death of the organism.

In this third and final stage, our digestion stops and our blood supply to the stomach lining lowers. As our stress continues, we cause very high levels of acidity and more digestive enzymes. Then we develop stress ulcers. When the stress continues, those ulcers will perforate and cause a medical catastrophe.

That's just the stomach! Our cardiovascular system also reacts to stress. As we continue with that stress, the heart, blood vessels and kidneys go through damage resulting in hypertension or heart disease.

As you can see, our self-induced stress eventually becomes responsible for us having strokes, heart attacks and hypertension – all of which are major causes of death in the Western world. And there is no need for it to be this way!

Quick check in regarding our own stress levels

OK, before we go any further, let's take a check on where we all are today with regards to stress. This is a simple test, which uses the Perceived Stress Scale (PSS) to determine how stressed we feel we are.

The Perceived Stress Scale (PSS) is a widely used psychological instrument designed to measure how much stress you perceive in your life. It doesn't assess objective stressors, but rather your individual interpretation and feelings about your current situation.

Developed by Sheldon Cohen and colleagues, the PSS consists of ten short questions that ask you to rate how often you felt or thought certain things in the past month. These questions tap into various aspects of stress perception, such as:

- Feeling unable to control things
- Things being unpredictable
- Feeling overloaded
- Feeling nervous or anxious

Each question uses a 4-point Likert scale, ranging from 0 ("Never") to 4 ("Very Often"). By adding up the scores for all questions, you get a total score between 0 and 40.

It's important to remember that these are just general guidelines, and individual experiences and stress responses can vary.

Benefits of using the PSS:

- Simple and easy to use: The self-report format makes it accessible to a wide audience.
- Reliable and valid: Extensive research supports its accuracy in measuring perceived stress.
- Brief and efficient: It takes only a few minutes to complete.
- Identifies areas of stress: Can help you pinpoint specific aspects of your life contributing to stress.

Perceived Stress Scale

The PSS is a classic stress assessment instrument. The tool, while originally developed in 1983, remains a popular choice for helping us understand how different situations affect our feelings and our perceived stress. The questions in this scale ask about your feelings and thoughts during the last month.

In each case, you will be asked to indicate how often you felt or thought a certain way. Although some of the questions are similar, there are differences between them and you should treat each one as a separate question. The best approach is to answer fairly quickly. That is, don't try to count the number of times you felt a particular way; rather, indicate the alternative that seems like a reasonable estimate.

Overall, the Perceived Stress Scale is a valuable tool for gaining insight into your personal stress levels and identifying areas where you might need to focus on stress management. If you're concerned about your stress levels, talking to a healthcare professional or mental health counsellor can be helpful.

For now, let's get started with the ten questions:

For each question choose from the following alternatives:

0 - never 1 - almost never 2 - sometimes 3 - fairly often 4 - very often

1. In the last month, how often have you been upset because of something that happened unexpectedly?

2. In the last month, how often have you felt that you were unable to control the important things in your life?

3. In the last month, how often have you felt nervous and stressed?

4. In the last month, how often have you felt confident about your ability to handle your personal problems?

5. In the last month, how often have you felt that things were going your way?

6. In the last month, how often have you found that you could not cope with all the things that you had to do?

7. In the last month, how often have you been able to control irritations in your life?

8. In the last month, how often have you felt that you were on top of things?

9. In the last month, how often have you been angered because of things that happened that were outside of your control?

10. In the last month, how often have you felt difficulties were piling up so high that you could not overcome them?

Figuring Your PSS Score

You can determine your PSS score by following these directions:

First, reverse your scores for questions 4, 5, 7, and 8. On these 4 questions, change the scores like this: 0 = 4, 1 = 3, 2 = 2, 3 = 1, 4 = 0.

Now add up your scores for each item to get a total.

My total score is __________.

Individual scores on the PSS can range from 0 to 40, with higher scores indicating higher perceived stress.

► Scores ranging from 0-13 would be considered low stress.

► Scores ranging from 14-26 would be considered moderate stress.

► Scores ranging from 27-40 would be considered high perceived stress.

The Perceived Stress Scale is interesting and important because your perception of what is happening in your life is most important. Consider the idea that two individuals could have had the exact same events and experiences in their lives for the past month. Depending on their perception, the total score could put one of those individuals in the low stress category and the total score could put the second person in the high stress category.

Addressing stress in older adults

For older adults, social connection is particularly important to reduce risk factors such as social isolation and loneliness. At this stage of life, meaningful social activities can significantly improve positive mental health, life satisfaction and quality of life; they can also reduce depressive symptoms. Example interventions include befriending initiatives, community and support groups, social skills training, creative arts groups, leisure and education services and volunteering programmes.

Protection from ageism and abuse is also critical. Key interventions include anti-discrimination policies and laws, educational interventions and intergenerational activities. A range of carer interventions – including respite care, advice, education, financial support and psychological interventions – can support carers to maintain a good and healthy caring relationship that avoids abuse of older people.

Stress caused by regret as we look back

As we age, it's natural to reflect on our lives and wonder what might have been. Sometimes, these reflections can lead to feelings of regret, a heavy burden that can weigh on our mental and emotional well-being.

One common source of regret is unfulfilled dreams. We may look back on our younger years and wish we had pursued a different path, taken more risks, or explored alternative opportunities.

These "what-if" scenarios can be haunting, leading to feelings of disappointment and sadness.

Another source of regret can be missed opportunities or relationships. We may regret not spending more time with loved ones, not taking that dream vacation, not pursuing a particular career path, or not having the desired relationship with another specific individual. These regrets can leave us feeling like we've missed out on something important.

Additionally, regrets can arise from mistakes or poor decisions we've made. We may look back on certain choices and wish we had done things differently. These regrets can be particularly painful, as they can make us feel like we've let ourselves down.

It's important to remember that regret is a normal human emotion. Everyone experiences it to some degree. However, dwelling on regrets can be detrimental to your mental health. It can lead to feelings of anxiety, depression, and self-blame.

To cope with regret, it's essential to practice self-compassion. Be kind to yourself and understand that everyone makes mistakes. Instead of focusing on what you could have done differently, focus on what you can do now to create a positive future. It's important to understand that the whole of our **life is simply a series of lessons we are destined to learn**.

It's also helpful to shift your perspective. Instead of dwelling on the past, try to focus on the present and the future. What can you do today to make your life better? What goals can you set for yourself?

Ageism in the workplace: A silent bias

Have you ever felt overlooked for a promotion or job opportunity? Have you been made to feel like your skills are outdated or that you're not as sharp as younger colleagues? If so, you might have experienced ageism.

It's important to recognise that ageism can manifest in various ways. Sometimes, it's overt, like being denied a job because of your age. Other times, it's more subtle, like being given less challenging assignments or excluded from important meetings.

Ageism can be particularly harmful because it can erode self-esteem and make it difficult to find new employment. It can also lead to financial hardship, as older workers may have fewer opportunities to increase their earnings.

While it's difficult to prove ageism, it's important to be aware of it and to speak up if you believe you're being discriminated against. Document any instances of ageism and consider seeking legal advice if necessary.

You have valuable skills and experience to offer. Don't let ageism hold you back. Keep learning, networking, and advocating for yourself. With the right mindset and strategies, you can thrive in the workplace, no matter your age.

Ageism is a widespread problem in the western world, affecting people of all ages. Studies have shown that:

In the United States, 20% of workers over 40 reported experiencing age discrimination in the workplace.

In Canada, 32% of older adults felt that their age was a barrier to employment.

In Australia, 40% of mature-aged workers believed that their age made it harder for them to find a job.

Ageism can manifest in various forms in the workplace, including:

Recruitment: Ageist stereotypes may lead to overlooking qualified older candidates during the selection process.

Training and development: Older workers may be excluded from training opportunities due to assumptions about their tech skills or adaptability.

Promotion: Biased perceptions about older workers' potential or energy levels can hinder their career advancement.

Redundancy: Age can be a factor in redundancy decisions, even if unfair or unfounded.

Workplace culture: Microaggressions, assumptions, and a lack of age-diverse role models can create a hostile environment for older workers.

Of course, you may be reading this and you may belong to a different culture, one that respects and cares for their ageing population. Ageism is linked to culture.

If there were a 'league table' of ageism linked to culture (which there should be) then where I am in the UK would be pretty high up on the list, whereas Sri Lanka is likely to be near the bottom of the list, that is, UK more ageist, Sri Lanka less ageist.

Ageism is most prevalent in individualistic countries like the United States, Germany, Ireland, South Africa, and Australia. Those countries tend to focus their identity on being independent and 'forward thinking.' In addition to having greater age biases, recent findings reveal that individualistic countries are more focused on maintaining youthful appearances.

Where ageism is highest, we see experienced people being replaced because of perceived cost differences – as well as working toward this youthful image. This is short-sighted and will end badly for the businesses that follow this reasoning. It is very difficult to replace someone with 40 years of experience with an apprentice.

What can we do? Hold our heads up and understand our own value. If you would like to continue working but opportunities in the workplace are passing you by, consider working for yourself. You have gazillions of transferrable skills you have collected through the years.

There are ideas on handling wealth coming up in Chapter 5 and ideas on creating wealth coming up in Chapter 6.

Treatment and care

Prompt recognition and treatment of mental health conditions in older adults is essential. This should follow standards for integrated care for older people, which is community-based and focused on both the long-term care of older adults living with mental health conditions and any decline in capacity.

Dementia is often an important concern. It affects people's mental health (for example, sparking symptoms of psychosis and depression), and requires access to quality mental health care.

My personal favourite way to stave off mental deterioration is meditation and walking in the countryside – sometimes at the same time.

Positive mindset

Whatever you choose, it's important to maintain a positive mindset. Very often, it is the dialogue in our head that causes our stress and anxiety. Our subconscious mind is telling us we are not good enough. This negative self-talk can spiral out of control, leading to feelings of inadequacy and worthlessness.

To combat this, we must learn to challenge these negative thoughts and replace them with positive affirmations. By consciously shifting our focus to the positive aspects of ourselves and our lives, we can begin to rewire our brains and reduce the impact of stress and anxiety.

This is a case of 'catching ourselves thinking', as mentioned before. We sense that we are having negative thoughts, feelings of overwhelm or anxiety and then we stop that thought pattern and replace it with a positive stream of thoughts. I did not find this easy at first, I admit. It is like a muscle, in that the more we practice, the stronger at it we become.

What we think about, we bring about. So constantly chewing over things and listening to our inner voice needs to stop.

For those of you who suffer from anxiety – it is okay to feel overwhelmed or anxious at times. These emotions are a normal part of the human experience. However, by practicing mindfulness, gratitude, and self-compassion, we can learn to manage these feelings in a healthy way.

From Victim to Victor

There is a large section of the population that live with a 'victim mindset'. That is, they believe that negative things are 'done to' them. People who think and feel this way are able to free themselves by catching those thoughts and reminding themselves that they have invented their world.

We are not the victims of the world in which we live – we are the creators.

If this describes you, stay alert to those thoughts as they come up and remind yourself that how you are thinking and feeling is creating your reality. Change those thoughts to positive and start to believe you are in control – because that is 100% true.

The love of Self

A great deal of stress and anxiety is self-inflicted. Have you ever told yourself, "This will be better when......" or "I will happier when.......

.....when I become famous....

.....when I get a new job....

.....when I meet the right person....

.....when I move home....

....when I lose weight....

....when I have more money....

....when I stop smoking/drinking....

All of these things that we are waiting to happen usually express a lack of self-love. Usually, these 'targets' we set ourselves show us where we are not loving ourselves.

We need to stop this 'future-gazing', love ourselves and set ourselves free. You will know when you have achieved this freedom when you simply accept yourself for what you are, regardless of what other people say.

You can believe the world is 'out to get you' or you can believe the world 'has your back'. Whichever you believe – that will be the case for you.

Albert Einstein said, "There are only two ways to live your life. One is as though nothing is a miracle. The other is as though everything is a miracle."

Everyone is looking for something, whether that is love, recognition, a sense of belonging. But what we're really after isn't the thing itself; it's the feeling we believe it will bring. The good news? That feeling is already within you. You don't have to wait for outside approval to know your worth. You exist, and that alone makes you valuable. You are part of something greater, connected to the Divine Creator.

That little voice feeding you fear and self-doubt, that's just your ego, recycling old worries and insecurities from the past. You don't have to listen. Instead, trust that the universe is working in your favour. You are wanted, you are loved, and your presence here matters more than you know. Look within yourself for the answer and stop berating yourself.

My own experience of stress – that led to anger

I can see now, looking back, that in the scenario I am going describe, I created the stress myself. And the stress I was under resulted in me being angry all the time.

Before I explain the scenario, I would like to point out that I'm not a doctor or psychiatrist – just someone who was born and brought up into anger and I'm speaking about my own experiences and my personal coping mechanisms. If you believe you have issues that are beyond the scope of this book, then I strongly recommend you contact your healthcare professional.

We are going to go through how we become stressed (then in my case, angry) how to stop it getting out of control and how to finally eliminate it. I'm explaining this in the hope that you and others you know and love will be better able to cope with stress.

I want to explain what I mean by anger because most people I speak with would declare themselves to be a non-angry person. And yet, that word covers everything from blind rage to mild resentment. That means it covers just about everyone you know and everyone you are ever likely to meet. Because most people will at least rise to mild resentment at some time in their lives.

At the lower end, anger includes sullenness, meanness, impatience, frustration and sarcasm, while at the higher end, it includes fury, jealousy, spite, hatred, aggression and violence. Most of us move through the spectrum at different times of our lives – and sometimes at different times of the day!

Anger provides a lot of energy, so we may feel energised when we are angry. So, we could say that anger has its place in certain circumstances, like getting yourself out of poverty. But then we need to learn to halt and let go of our anger. Because there is a great deal of anger in the world right now.

The amount of suppressed anger within our world population is reflected in how much violence is in our media. We are presented with others who let out their anger in the form of beatings, shootings, stabbings and killings.

We live in a world where we are constantly being shown 'chronic resentment' through our media channels. We are led to believe that one nation has 'wronged' another nation and we become collectors of injustices.

Also, we feel so much guilt about our anger that we need to justify it by making the object of our anger "wrong" so that we can tell ourselves our anger is "justified." That's right, we think we are justified in being angry.

We have defined who or what is"wrong" and we get a small, cheap satisfaction from that – but the price we pay for anger is sickness and premature death.

My stress build-up to my 'red mist'

In 2017 I was taking the role of full-time carer for my wife, who has Parkinson's and MS. I was also running my own small business and doing all the cleaning, shopping, cooking, laundry and everything else that needed doing in the house and garden - plus being the number one carer for my wife.

I remember the day this all became too much for me.

I was complaining to my wife about how tough it was all getting and that I felt I needed some help. I'd already been to see her doctor to see if the health service provided support and was told no. I also saw my own doctor and asked him what I should be doing. I remember his answer: "Most people in your position just bugger off. If you keep stepping forward to help your wife, the Health Service will keep stepping back."

Now, back to that fateful day in the kitchen with my wife. I think I must have gone through all the reasons I objected to being left in the role I found myself in and I explained that the stress I was under was killing me.

As I set out each element of my grievances, my anger moved up to another level. I could feel my rage building and I felt perfectly justified in telling my wife how I felt and letting off steam as I went along. It was not the fault of my wife that I found myself in this position and I really don't know what I expected her to do about any of it – but I continued to become more angry.

Eventually I found myself so angry that I could no longer speak.

The emotions were swirling around inside me and by then, even my ranting was not placating me in any way.

This was the point when I morphed from being a carer to my wife into being a threat to my wife. Not a physical threat – but not someone on whom she could rely. From Mr Dependable to Mr Angry Person. From Doctor Jekyll to Mister Hyde.

My face was red, my heart rate sky high and my system coursing with negative chemicals. I realised that my ranting was not resolving anything so, in frustration, I stopped and left the room.

That situation eventually got resolved. I realised that my wife was not getting the care at home that she needed if I was angry all the time. It became obvious that we needed someone to join us in the home to take care of her. But it was going to cost. I decided to simply work harder, earn more money and pay someone to look after my wife, something I was clearly not managing very well.

It has only been during the last couple of years that I have come to understand what happens to the chemicals in our brain that are produced when we are angry.

One of the shining lights has been reading “Letting Go” by David Hawkins.

How to self-help

These days I know the underlying stress is there that will mature into anger. But I am getting better at catching myself thinking of being angry – and by doing that I can stop it. This is not easy at first. I have learned to “listen” to my thoughts. We can monitor ourselves and be our own ‘observer’. Then, when we start thinking about something that is making us angry, we can stop it and change our way of thinking – well before we break down into anger. We can simply accept the thing that is making us cross – and let it go.

In my case, once I realise I am stressed and it is working me up into anger, I stop and focus on breathing. Please do this exercise now, as you read. It will be a 3 second inhale, pause, then a 3 second exhale – repeated 3 times.

OK, breathe in, two, three, - pause - and then out two, three.

Then the same sequence again – in, two three, pause and out two three.

And in 2, 3, pause, out 2, 3.

By switching your thinking from your brain – where the anger is – to your core functions like breathing – you can release the anger before it takes hold. I find that when I realise the stress is building – and I catch myself – just the first breath is enough to ‘break the cycle.’ The subsequent breaths simply help relax me further. And we can all follow this method when we feel we are becoming ‘swamped’ with stress.

However, that's not the end. We need to let go of the anger otherwise it's just another suppressed feeling – and we all have lots of those. What I do is think, "why does this make me angry?" And then I can work out where it might have started.

As an example, let's take another driving analogy, a common occurrence on the road. A driver cuts in front of me on a busy road. Immediately I feel angry. I breathe and stop it escalating. Then I look back at what caused the anger. I was brought up to believe life was a "fight" a "race" – something I had to win. Winning was to be achieved above anything, including putting other people down. But now I know I'm mature enough that I don't need that old belief and I can let it go.

So, I can now think, "that driver is in a hurry because it's an emergency for him. Help him by getting out of his way. I am not in a race with him." Now, I don't feel hurt by his action. Now I have a positive feeling that I'm helping someone. It's all a matter of perception – **and we can change how we perceive things**.

Another way I help myself to alleviate stress is to meditate each morning. That way, when I feel any distress rising in me, I can go back to that calm place I was in earlier in the day and just do some breathing exercises. It usually lasts less than ten seconds. I know from experience that we can catch ourselves before our stressful emotions run away with us and take a few seconds to stop and breathe.

That means we can all handle this ourselves. No need to call emergency services or phone a friend. **We are just one breath away from reducing our stress**.

That will result in better personal relationships and better health.

Some basic tips on reducing stress

An article seen in The Times, July 29, 2023 (abbreviated here)

"Nine out of ten of us feel under pressure at some point every day, according to a recent survey of 2,000 adults — and we deal with stress in very different ways. The poll found that among the de-stressing methods people found most effective was the simple act of having a cup of tea — a much more popular choice than yoga or meditation. But which everyday de-stressors really do lower cortisol, heart rate and tension in the body? Here's what the experts say are the best anxiety-busters:

Curl up with a good book

Reading a good book for as little as six minutes can reduce stress by 68 per cent by distracting the brain from anxious and stressful thinking, lowering heart rate and muscle tension, according to research at the University of Sussex.

Have a 'podcast walk'

Listening to podcasts or audio books can have a powerful effect on reducing stress levels. It is suggested that we walk in silence, while listening to a Ted talk or to upbeat music.

Go for a 15-minute run

Running is among the best tension-busters and heading out for even a short run can boost levels of endorphins and endocannabinoids — biochemical substances similar to cannabis naturally produced by the body, known to enhance mood. Studies have shown improvement after jogging by as much as 87 per cent, with the researchers concluding that running helps to "improve mental health by facilitating oxygen supply to the brain and eliminating waste products from the body".

Put the kettle on

Having a nice cuppa ranks highly as a de-stressor and there's scientific evidence to back up the belief that tea reduces feelings of anxiety. Making and drinking tea have been shown to result in lower levels of the stress hormone cortisol, according to research from University College London. An amino acid in tea, called L-theanine, is also known to relax the mind without making you drowsy.

Chill out! Put ice packs on the face or neck

There's growing evidence that cold-water swimming or a cold shower can help to reduce anxiety. When cold receptors on human skin are activated by exposure to cold water, it triggers electrical impulses to the brain that are believed to have a stress-lowering effect. But if the prospect of a dip leaves you cold, you could try holding ice packs or ice cubes to your face or neck. This restricts blood vessels, which in turn stimulates the vagus nerve responsible for calming. Your heart rate speeds up during stress but applying ice packs to the neck was shown to slow heart rate in one study at the University of Luxembourg.

Listen to loud music

You might assume that soothing music is the route to a calm mind, but counterintuitively, researchers have shown that blasting out rock tunes can provide a form of stress relief. Exposing people to what Australian psychologists called "extreme music", such as heavy metal and punk, for ten minutes helped people to process and regulate feelings of anger and tension, according to a recent study published in the Frontiers in Human Neuroscience journal.

Hands in the air!

Any kind of dancing has the power to release tension. "The many movements of dance activate the vagus nerve, which has a calming effect on the mind," says the psychologist and neuroscientist Dr Julia Christensen, author of Dancing Is the Best Medicine (Greystone Books). "Raising your hands above your head when you dance helps to open the lungs, make breathing more efficient and relaxing the muscles of the diaphragm located between belly and chest, where we tend to hold tension that leaves us feeling anxious."

Do some gardening — a few times a week

Getting out into the garden twice a week can do wonders for your stress levels, according to researchers from the University of Sheffield's Department of Landscape Architecture and the Royal Horticultural Society. But the more often you do it, the better — the study found that people who garden even for a short time every day have lower stress levels than people who do no gardening at all.

Take a B6 vitamin supplement

Dr David Field, a researcher in the school of psychology and clinical language sciences at the University of Reading, compared the effects of taking a supplement of vitamin B6 — known to increase the body's production of gamma-aminobutyric acid, a chemical that blocks impulses between nerve cells in the brain — or vitamin B12, a deficiency of which has been associated with depression. He discovered that while vitamin B12 capsules were no better than a placebo at boosting the mood of participants, a supplement of vitamin B6 brought considerable benefits.

Lift weights and do some lunges

It's not just aerobic exercise such as running and cycling that can leave you on a high. Weight training and lunges can combat anxiety, according to a study at the University of Limerick involving 1,877 participants. In a trial 28 young adults were asked to follow a basic plan of lunges, lifts, squats and crunches, sometimes using weights, for two months — anxiety levels in tests dropped by 20 per cent in the weight trainers compared with a control group.

Take a vitamin D supplement

Low vitamin D levels have been associated with increased symptoms of anxiety in some studies, and supplementing with the vitamin has been shown to have a beneficial effect on brain and mood in people who are deficient, according to a team from China reporting in Brain and Behaviour journal. "Good concentrations of vitamin D support adequate concentrations of neurotransmitters in the brain that boost feelings of wellbeing," says Ian Marber, a nutrition therapist. "Vitamin D is made naturally by the body on exposure to sunlight, so getting outside is important, but a 10mcg supplement is recommended during the winter months."

Meet up with or phone a friend

Spending time with friends can improve mood and lower stress levels. Just one conversation with a friend — preferably in person, although phone and online chats were beneficial too — was enough to make a positive difference to mood according to Jeffrey Hall, professor of communication studies at the University of Kansas in a report in the Communication Research journal.

Have a cuddle

Hugging a friend, relative or partner reduces stress and may even protect against infections, according to research from Carnegie Mellon University in Pennsylvania. Women may benefit more than men, however, according to a team of German scientists last year. Their findings in the journal Plos One showed that women in their study who hugged a partner before a stressful situation displayed a significant reduction in the production of the stress hormone cortisol, whereas the men did not.

Just ten minutes of massage can help you to relax deeply

If all you can manage is ten minutes of doing nothing, it will, of course, make a difference to your stress levels. Psychologists reporting in the journal Scientific Reports showed that people who sat down and relaxed for ten minutes reported much higher levels of psychological and physiological relaxation. The benefits were even greater if they received a head and neck massage in that time.

Spend ten minutes with a dog (it doesn't have to be yours)

Even if you don't have a dog, spending time with one could lower your stress levels. In their Paws for Thought study in 2019, psychologists at the University of Warwick showed that stressed-out students who spent ten minutes with a dog experienced "considerably reduced anxiety and feelings of sadness, and improved happiness scores".

Eat more apples and pears

Processed foods and sugary drinks are the worst thing you can eat for dealing with stress. Wholegrains, pulses, fruit and vegetables contain valuable nutrients that can help us to combat anxiety. An Australian study last year showed that the more fresh produce consumed by middle-aged people, the lower their levels of perceived stress. Those who ate the most apples and pears, oranges and bananas were least likely to consider themselves highly stressed.

Go for a walk

A ten-minute walk lowers stress and anxiety as effectively as meditating for the same amount of time, according to exercise scientists from the University of Mississippi. For best results, walk in a park or wood. German researchers reporting in the Molecular Psychiatry journal found that activity in the brain regions involved in processing stress decreased more significantly after a one-hour walk in nature than in a busy city.

Allow yourself one glass of wine

An occasional drink may help you unwind, according to a study from Massachusetts General Hospital. Researchers found that those who had a light to moderate alcohol intake — that's no more than one drink, such as a small glass of wine a day for women and one or two daily drinks a day for men — produced reduced stress signals in the amygdala, the part of the brain associated with stress responses, compared with those who drank little or nothing.

Looking at leaves or shells can calm you down in less than a minute

Absorbing yourself in fractals, the repetitive patterns and shapes of nature that appear on leaves, trees and shells, can help to reduce acute stress in as little as 60 seconds, according to research by psychologists from Lund University in Sweden and the University of Oregon. When we study fractals it produces an increase of alpha wave frequency in the frontal areas of the brain, promoting feelings of calm and wellbeing, researchers have shown.

Have a soak in the bath twice a week

Having a nice long soak in the bath can provide a mood lift that lasts if you do it regularly, according to researchers at the University of Freiburg. Over eight weeks, participants with moderate depression were asked to take a 40°C bath for up to half an hour twice a week or to take part in two 45 to 50-minute aerobic workouts. Results showed the positive, stress-reducing benefits of bathing were similar to those of moderate intensity exercise, such as brisk walking or jogging.

Get baking

Small creative tasks such as baking cakes have been shown to reduce stress and boost mood in a study by researchers at the University of Minnesota, reporting in The Journal of Positive Psychology. "Baking can absorb and connect you with a sense of stillness and calm," Dr Jennifer Wild, consultant clinical psychologist and associate professor at the University of Oxford, says.

Keep a diary — get things off your chest by writing them down

Writing things down — good and bad — can help to reduce stress. Psychologists at the University of Northumbria, in a study in 2018, asked one group of people to write about "the most wonderful experiences of their life" and another to write about a neutral experience while measuring levels of anxiety before and after the task. Results showed that anxiety levels were not only lower after writing about the positive experiences but stayed lower for up to four weeks. Wild says that getting things off your chest at the end of the day by writing down negative thoughts can be beneficial too. "Writing down your worries helps you to keep track of them and helps people to realise that most things people fear or are anxious about don't happen," she says.

Tidy a cupboard or drawer

It pays to keep things tidy. Putting away clutter helps you to think more clearly, according to psychologists at Princeton University who found that it affects our ability to focus. Another paper by researchers in California, published in Personality and Social Psychology Bulletin, showed that people living in messy houses had higher levels of cortisol.

Go for a swim

Water acts as a giant cushion for our bodies, protecting our joints and soothing our minds. A few years ago, a survey by the swimwear manufacturer Speedo revealed that 74 per cent of swimmers find the activity helps to release pent-up stress and tension. A 2018 YouGov poll, commissioned by Swim England, reported that a regular swim has reduced anxiety and stress for 1.4 million Britons. A relaxing, low-effort swim is perfect for reducing stress.

Switch off your phone for half an hour

We often turn to digital devices to de-stress, but they often make matters worse. In 2023, psychiatrists from Iran reporting in the BMC Psychiatry journal found that overreliance on smartphones raised stress and anxiety levels in university students. Switching off your digital devices can be a helpful way to unwind. “You can train your mind to live without your phone and tablet,” Wild says. “Start by giving yourself a complete 30-minute break every day and gradually build up the phone-free time to an hour a day.”

Summary

So, we have spoken of mental wellbeing and discovered that it’s more than just the absence of mental illness. It's a state of positive mental health that allows us to navigate life's ups and downs with resilience.

We know intuitively that when we're in a good mental state, we are more able to handle stress, solve problems, and build strong relationships. We're more likely to make healthy choices, pursue our passions, and have good friends in our lives.

We discovered once more that how we are thinking and feeling determines the outcomes in our lives. It is of the utmost importance that we maintain a positive mindset. Only dwell on the present moment. We cannot alter the past and we are creating the future in this moment.

Maintain a sense of wellbeing

The effects of our mental health are experienced in every aspect of our lives. Our moods, physical health, and social connections all play a role in how we cope with adversity and unexpected hurdles.

When we're in a positive mental state, we're more likely to make healthy choices, build strong relationships, and find meaning in life. We're better equipped to handle challenges and bounce back from setbacks.

We also looked at the effect that stress has on the human body and how there are 'negative' chemicals produced (adrenaline and cortisol). We saw that those chemicals would naturally subside but that we humans keep going through the experience in our minds, thereby perpetuating the effect of the trauma we experienced.

Some reminders from everything we covered:

Prioritise self-care: Make time for activities that you enjoy and that help you relax. This could include exercise, hobbies, or spending time in nature.

Build strong relationships: Connect with friends, family, and loved ones. Social connections can provide emotional support and a sense of belonging.

Practice mindfulness: Mindfulness techniques like meditation and deep breathing can help reduce stress and improve focus.

Seek professional help: If you're struggling with mental health issues, don't hesitate to reach out to a therapist or counsellor.

Mental health is just as important as physical health. By taking care of your mind, you're investing in your overall well-being and creating a brighter future.

Importance of relationships on mental wellbeing

You are a social creature. You thrive on connection, whether it's with family, friends, or romantic partners. Your relationships play a vital role in your mental and emotional well-being. When you have strong social connections, you feel less isolated and more supported. You have people to turn to when you need help, advice, or simply a listening ear. These connections provide a sense of belonging and purpose.

Relationships can provide a buffer against stress. When we're feeling overwhelmed, having someone to talk to can help us see things from a different perspective.

Positive relationships can also boost our self-esteem. Knowing that we are valued and loved by others can help us feel good about ourselves. It can give us the confidence to pursue our goals and overcome challenges.

And it is with that in mind that we leave it here and move straight into personal relationships in the next chapter.

Chapter 4 – Personal Relationships

"The most beautiful thing in life is to see a person you love smiling. And even more beautiful is that you are the reason behind it."

Source unknown

Friends are like gold, and they get even more precious as we get older. Neighbours, family, and friends are your personal cheerleaders, your listening ears, and your partners in crime for new adventures. They're the ones who'll share your laughs when you're happy and support you on those odd occasions when you're not feeling well.

We humans seem to have an inherent need to belong to a "tribe." It's as if it's hard-wired from our early cave-dwelling ancestors. Being part of a community provides a sense of security, belonging, and purpose. Our relationships with others help to define who we are.

Friendships offer a wealth of benefits. They provide emotional support, companionship, and a sense of belonging. They can help us to reduce stress, improve our mental health, and even live longer.

Friends are there to celebrate our successes and offer comfort in times of hardship. They're the ones who will pick us up when we fall down and help us see the bright side of things.

As we get older, our friendships may change. Some may fade away, while others may deepen. And, as we get older our relationships matter to us much more for the stability they bring.

So, cherish your friendships my friend! Nurture them, cultivate them, and appreciate the invaluable gift they bring to your life.

Subjects in this chapter:

- Why relationships matter after 60
- Loneliness and what we can do about it
- Cherishing your partner
- Finding a romantic relationship after 60

When I think of personal relationships in later life, I can't help thinking about the situation my mother was in at the end of her life. She seemed to me to be surrounded by friends she had known for many decades.

The council estate in Middlesbrough where I was brought up is called Berwick Hills. I know, sounds glamorous, doesn't it – like Beverley Hills or Hollywood Hills? Well, it was a long way from either of them.

But what it had in abundance was an ethos of looking after each other. By the time my mother reached pensionable age, she was immobilised through arthritis, all of us six children had flown the nest and my father had been long gone, having been taken by a heart attack aged 56. Our family had lived in that council house since it was built and by the time my mother passed away, she had been there over 45 years. Neighbours tend to be long-term in rented council provided accommodation, since the life-style choices of those families are extremely limited. So, most of my mother's friends were literally on her doorstep.

This meant that people we had grown up with became very close with my mother. They would check on her, run small errands and bring food to her. Once, when I was about 35 and paying her a visit, I was sitting in my mother's front room when lunch was served by Mrs Smith from over the road. It was a large plate full of what seemed like half a roast chicken with vegetables and a Yorkshire pudding. As soon as the kind neighbour left, my mother handed the tray over to me and said, "Eat that for me please Peter, I want to be able to hand her a plate back that's been cleared."

Other times, I would be speaking with my mother when a neighbour would come in through the back door and just appear in the front room unannounced, either bringing something my mother asked for or taking a request for something my mother needed.

The kindness of her friends who lived in and around our road was very touching. They would be on alert for signs of health issues and be there to keep her company. There were health scares. The neighbours would contact one of my two sisters, who both lived closer than us four boys.

I appreciate that we don't all have that luxury of friends in the road in which we live to bring us comfort as we age. But we can all work toward that goal by starting to make friends with our neighbours. Starting with us helping them. In my life, I have found that if we want help from someone, we have to be prepared to help them first.

The Silver Lining

I just want to touch on retirement here because lots of us have developed work friends and those friendships are in jeopardy when we leave. We will discuss retirement with regard to work and the options we have to continue to work – if we wish – later in the book. For now though, this is about relationships.

Retirement could mean sitting at home reading the newspaper but it's a chance to hit the reset button and redefine what life means to you. You need to make an effort. Stay in touch with your old work buddies, reconnect with old friends that you may have let slip, be more friendly with neighbours.

Retirement is also a chance to give back to your community, to volunteer, to mentor younger generations. Think about how you would like to 'donate' your time, after all, you will have a lot of it to fill. And each of the above suggestions will lead to you building even more relationships.

Please do not forget that you have a story to tell. Most people are interested in hearing about what life was like 60 or 70 years ago. Treat the wrinkles on your face as a badge of honour – like the annual rings of a tree that define its age.

The magic of connections

Human beings are social creatures. We thrive on connection, whether it's with family, friends, or romantic partners. Our relationships are like a warm blanket on a cold day, providing comfort, support, and a sense of belonging.

When we have strong social connections, we're less likely to feel lonely or isolated. We have people to turn to when we need a listening ear.

Studies have shown that people with strong social connections are less likely to suffer from depression, anxiety, and other mental health issues. They're also more likely to live longer.

Relationships can provide a buffer against stress. When we're feeling overwhelmed, having someone to talk to can help us see things from a different perspective. Our loved ones can offer support, encouragement, and a shoulder to cry on.

Positive relationships can also boost our self-esteem. Knowing that we are valued and loved by others can help us feel good about ourselves. It can give us the confidence to pursue our goals and overcome challenges.

So, the next time you're feeling down, reach out to a friend or loved one. You might be surprised at how much better you feel after a good conversation. Strong relationships are a valuable asset, and they're worth investing in.

Positive health effects of social connections

According to a recent study by Nottingham Trent University, having strong social connections can improve your health. This research was done during the Covid-19 pandemic.

"The research recommends that public health messaging focus on smaller networks as well as multiple groups, particularly in times of crisis when individuals should be encouraged to share their positive health behaviours with their close social circles.

It is also suggested that healthcare systems can reduce the reliance on pharmaceutical treatments by using social prescribing to support individuals who do not have these bonds in their life.

The results of the study, which included a broad range of countries such as Bangladesh, Brazil and Peru, have implications for tackling negative physical and mental health effects from a global perspective. The study goes beyond the remit of traditional approaches in psychology by reaching so much of the global population.

Anthropologist at the University of Kent, Dr Martha Newson, said: "This research speaks to the universal need to belong – this is one of the reasons we felt it was so important to include a truly diverse sample from across the globe. Wherever you are in the world, other people matter to you."

"We found that having lots of groups was important to encourage better health behaviours, including bonding to abstract groups like your country or government, but most important of all are our closest friends and family — groups that we have likely recognised as being important since the beginning of human history."

Assistant Professor at the Centre for Trust, Peace, and Social Relations at Coventry University, Dr Valerie van Mulukom, added: "In the West, we tend to think of ourselves as individuals who have to survive and conquer the world on our own. Our research demonstrates that in fact, humans are very much social animals, who benefit from, and rely on, their communities in more ways than one. In challenging times, this is even more pronounced. It is advisable for government policies to consider these psychological needs and mechanisms and involve local authorities and grassroots organisations for maximum efficiency and wellbeing in times of disaster."

Now, we are not just talking about feeling good; there's actual science behind this. Studies have shown that having strong social ties can boost your immune system and lower your stress levels. It's like having a secret weapon against ageing! There is evidence that when you have an active social life, there is more chance of you living longer.

When you're surrounded by people who care about you, you feel less alone. You're more likely to take care of yourself, both physically and mentally. Sharing your thoughts and feelings with someone you trust can be a huge relief, and it helps you to see things from a different perspective.

Loneliness

Whatever the reasons for you feeling lonely, know that it is a normal human experience and there are steps you can take right now to help alleviate loneliness, protect your health, and strengthen your connections with others

Something I have seen that may be useful for you is the exercise on the following page.

Exercise - "Letter to Loneliness"

Materials: Paper, pen.

Instructions: Write a letter to your loneliness as if it were a person. Explore what it feels like, when it appears, and what you think it needs. This isn't about banishing loneliness but understanding it better.

Reflection: This exercise can be very cathartic. It helps you externalise your feelings and gain a deeper understanding of the roots of your loneliness.

The exercise is meant for self-reflection and exploration. There are no "right" or "wrong" answers.

If the exercise brings up difficult emotions, it might be helpful to talk to a therapist or counsellor.

Loneliness in older people

The following information is taken from a UK NHS website regarding mental health and particularly elderly people being lonely. It's included here because it sets out stark figures and states the problem very well. And, hopefully, it will prompt you to do some research of your own.

"Older people are especially vulnerable to loneliness and social isolation – and it can have a serious effect on health." But there are ways to overcome loneliness, even if you live alone and find it hard to get out.

Hundreds of thousands of elderly people are lonely and cut off from society in this country, especially those over the age of 75.

According to Age UK, more than 2 million people in England over the age of 75 live alone, and more than a million older people say they go over a month without speaking to a friend, neighbour or family member.

People can become socially isolated for a variety of reasons, such as getting older or weaker, no longer being the hub of their family, leaving the workplace, the deaths of spouses and friends, or through disability or illness.

Whatever the cause, it's shockingly easy to be left feeling alone and vulnerable, which can lead to depression and a serious decline in physical health and wellbeing.

Someone who's lonely probably also finds it hard to reach out. There's a stigma surrounding loneliness, and older people tend not to ask for help because they have too much pride.

It's important to remember loneliness can – and does – affect anyone, of any age.

Here are ways for older people to connect with others and feel useful and appreciated again.

Smile, even if it feels hard

Grab every chance to smile at others or begin a conversation – for instance, with the cashier at the shop or the person next to you in the GP waiting room. Personally, this is an area in which I should try harder. I am usually happy and sometimes making jokes – but I don't smile very much. **This is the number one life lesson: smiling.**

If you're shy or not sure what to say, try asking people about themselves – and speak with a smile on your face!

Smiling is more than just a facial expression; it's a powerful tool for connecting with others and improving our overall well-being. It's a universal language that transcends cultural boundaries.

When we smile, we release endorphins, our body's natural feel-good chemicals. These endorphins can help reduce stress, boost our mood, and even alleviate physical pain. If you are feeling a bit low, try cracking a smile – it might just surprise you how much better you feel.

Smiling is also contagious. When we see someone smiling, it's natural for us to smile back. This creates a positive feedback loop that can spread joy and happiness throughout a community.

Moreover, smiling can make us appear more approachable and friendly. It's a nonverbal cue that says, "I'm open to connection." This can help us build stronger relationships and make new friends.

Smiling can also boost our self-confidence. When we smile, we feel more positive about ourselves and our abilities. This can help us overcome challenges and achieve our goals.

Invite friends for tea

If you're feeling down and alone, it's tempting to think nobody wants to visit you. But often friends, family and neighbours will appreciate receiving an invitation to come and spend some time with you. As mentioned earlier, if you are thinking you would like to be invited to a friend or neighbour's house – invite them to yours first.

Keep in touch by phone

Having a chat with a friend or relative over the phone can be the next best thing to being with them. Remember their birthday and send them a card as well as calling them.

Learn to love computers

If your friends and family live far away, a good way to stay in touch, especially with grandchildren, is by using a personal computer, smartphone or tablet.

You can share emails and photos with family and friends, have free video chats using services such as Zoom, FaceTime or Viber, and make new online "friends" or reconnect with old friends on social media sites such as Facebook, Instagram or Twitter and website forums.

A smartphone or tablet can be especially useful if you can't get around very easily, as you can sit with it on your knee or close to hand and the screen is clear and bright.

A sponge-tip stylus pen or speech recognition may help if the touchscreen is difficult for arthritic hands or fingers with poor circulation.

Libraries and community centres often hold regular training courses for older people to learn basic computer skills – as well as being a good place to meet and spend time with others in their own right. For example, our village hall has a group of 'Silver Surfers', where these online skills are taught for free. And once you become adept, join the team of instructors and make more new friends.

Get involved in local community activities

These will vary according to where you live, but the chances are you'll have access to a singing or walking group, book clubs, bridge, bingo, quiz nights and faith groups.

Not to mention local branches of regional and national organisations that hold social events, such as the Women's Institute and Re-engage.

The Silver Line helpline (0800 470 8090) can let you know what's going on in your local area.

Fill your diary

It can help you feel less lonely if you plan the week ahead and put things in your diary to look forward to each day, such as a walk in the park or going to a local coffee shop, library, sports centre, cinema or museum.

Independent Age has published a guide about what to do if you're feeling lonely, which includes tips about activities you could try.

Get out and about

Don't wait for people to come and see you – travel to visit them.

One advantage of being older is that public transport is better value. Local bus travel is free for older people across England (though remoter areas may have more limited bus services).

The age at which you can apply for your free bus pass depends on when you were born and where you live.

Contact your local authority for more information on how to apply.

Help others

Use the knowledge and experience you have gained over a lifetime to give something back to your community.

You'll get lots back in return, such as new skills and confidence – and, usually, some new friends, too.

There are endless volunteering opportunities that relish the qualities and skills of older people, such as patience, experience and calmness.

Examples are Home-Start, Sure Start, helping in a local charity shop or hospital or with a school reading programme. You can also volunteer to help the Citizens Advice charity in a range of activities.

Join the University of the Third Age

The University of the Third Age (U3A) operates in many areas, offering older people the chance to learn or do something new.

Run by volunteers, U3A has no exams. Instead, it gives you the chance to do, play or learn something you may never have done before, or something you haven't considered since your school days.

U3A is also a great place to meet people and make new friends.

It's all a matter of mindset

Back to our recurring theme! When we sit alone and tell ourselves we are lonely, that is the life we will create for ourselves. We all appreciate it can be a problem. And we all have the solution inside ourselves.

I have already covered the benefits of meditation. This is how we can sit quietly and contemplate what we want our lives to be. We are creating our lives from our subconscious every minute of every day. This is our chance to create whatever we want. Set a positive frame of mind, smile and be grateful for everything you have in life.

Giving back to your neighbourhood

In my own case, I have volunteered to sit on the committee for our Village Society, run the Neighbourhood Watch scheme for the road I live in, and stepped up to challenge local planning applications – where I did not believe it was in the best interests of the village. And I've challenged local businesses, when they have been responsible for polluting our natural surroundings.

I did this because I could see that someone needed to step up. What I hadn't realised is that my involvement in the village means that I am reasonably well known locally and this helps when I need someone to step up for me.

Recently we had a fire at home. It was on the scaffolding boards that were on the outside of the house because the roof was being replaced. It could easily have spread to the roof, which had the tiles removed so the wooden frame of the roof was exposed. At 4am, a neighbour woke and looked out of her window and saw the fire at my house. She called the fire service and ran down the avenue shouting, "help, fire" and other neighbours came out of their homes to see how they might assist.

At least five families had someone standing in the road watching the events unfurl, standing ready to help. I was outside with my garden hose pointed at the scaffolding boards. The fire service was here in a matter of minutes and quickly put the fire out.

I like to think that my wife being in a wheelchair and my volunteering in the local community helped to prompt friendly support from my neighbours. They all know I would be there for them.

Cognitive benefits

Studies suggest strong social connections can reduce the risk of cognitive decline. Keeping your brain active is just as important as keeping your body moving. And believe it or not, chatting with friends is a fantastic brain workout!

Every conversation is a little puzzle, figuring out what the other person is thinking, and finding the right words to share your thoughts. It's like mental gymnastics, without the sweaty clothes.

Physical health advantages

Research indicates that strong social connections can improve physical health and even increase longevity.

It's no secret that having good friends is great for your soul, but it's also fantastic for your physical health. Research from Harvard School of Public Health shows that people with strong social connections tend to live longer and healthier lives.

The link to that research is here:

An active social life may help you live longer | News - HSPH. Harvard.edu www.tiny.cc/eqtc001

When you're surrounded by people who care about you, it helps to keep you on track with things like eating right and getting enough exercise. Plus, laughing with friends is like a natural mood booster, and we all know that feeling good does wonders for your overall health. Get involved in as many social gatherings as you can. It's not just about having fun, it's about giving your body and mind a big health boost.

Redefining friendships

Friendships tend to get better with age. As we move past 60, these bonds often deepen.

I have found that now I'm more mature, I start to share my hopes, fears, and dreams with a level of openness that comes with experience. I also understand more about the importance of showing our vulnerabilities. When people can see that we are 'only human' and that we also have issues, they will warm to us and usually share their vulnerabilities.

It's amazing how our priorities can change. Shared experiences, like raising kids or building careers, might fade into the background, making space for new interests and connections. Maybe you discover a shared love of gardening, or a passion for walking in the countryside. These shared activities can bring you even closer.

And let's not forget about the joy of simply enjoying each other's company. Whether it's a weekly coffee catch-up, a shared hobby, or just sitting in comfortable silence, these moments are precious. These late-life friendships are often built on trust, respect, and a deep understanding.

If you did have the experience of raising kids, perhaps there are parents of youngsters in your street that you could relate with. Just two doors away from me are a family with two small children. Their children are an elder boy of school age and younger girl of kindergarten age – exactly the same as my grandchildren who live in Dubai. I have shown photographs of my two grandchildren to the parents two doors away. This allows me a certain grace in speaking with their children because I have explained why I love engaging with all children and specifically theirs. Now it's OK to make a small gift for each of them at Christmas. That means both parents stop to speak with me whenever we pass in the avenue.

Another observation on friends is that old friends see you as you were. The people that you make friends with from now will only see you as you are. And you can start being the person you always wanted to be!

My advice? – get out more!

Reaching 60 can be a time of great change, and sometimes, our social circles can shrink along with our work schedules. But it's never too late to make new friends.

Joining a club or group based on your interests is a fantastic way to meet like-minded people. Whether you're a bookworm, a gardener, or a dance enthusiast, there's a group out there for you. Taking up a new hobby or class can also be a great way to expand your social circle. Learning something new is not only stimulating but also a great conversation starter.

And if the club or special interest group that you would like to join does not exist in your area – start one!

Another idea might be to get a dog. Children and animals are great icebreakers. Wherever you may go for a dog walk, there are sure to be other people like you and you already have a shared interest. Don't wait for them to speak to you – ask them about their dog.

Something that I started in my 60s is beekeeping. I have two honeybee colonies in my back garden. I've joined the local beekeeping association and we meet twice a year, in summer and at Christmas, where we all bring our own food and drink. I have made new friends through beekeeping. And I always make a friend when I gift my honey to someone. Beekeeping also keeps you mentally agile, since you will never be as smart as a honeybee.

Online communities

And let's not forget about technology! Online platforms and social media groups can connect you with people who have similar interests, no matter where you live.

An online community refers to a group of individuals who interact and engage with one another through online platforms, websites, and on social media. These communities are formed around shared interests, goals, or affiliations, and they provide a digital space for people to connect, collaborate, and communicate.

How do online communities work? Online communities can take various forms, such as forums, discussion boards, social media groups, or specialised platforms. They enable individuals from diverse geographical locations to come together, exchange information, share ideas, seek support, or participate in discussions centred around their common interests.

What happens in online communities? Within an online community, members can engage in conversations, ask questions, offer advice, share experiences, or provide resources related to the community's topic or theme. These communities foster a sense of belonging, enable connections between like-minded individuals, and often cultivate a supportive environment for users to interact and learn from one another.

Online communities play a vital role in connecting people who may not have access to similar communities in their immediate physical surroundings. They offer opportunities for networking, knowledge sharing, and social interaction, ultimately creating a sense of virtual community where individuals can connect and engage with others who share their passions or goals.

Staying in contact using technology

Whilst we are speaking of online - technology has brought us closer together, even when we're miles apart. Video calls are like having a window into someone else's life. It's the next best thing to being there. You can see their smiles, hear their laughter, and even share a cup of virtual coffee. Social media is another great way to stay connected.

And let's not forget about messaging apps. They're perfect for quick check-ins, sharing funny stories, or just sending a simple "I'm thinking of you" message. It's a small thing, but it can make a big difference. So, embrace the tech and stay connected with your loved ones, no matter the distance.

Cherishing connections and showing gratitude

It’s easy to get caught up in the daily hustle, but taking a moment to appreciate the people who colour your world is essential. Friends, family, and even casual acquaintances enrich our lives in countless ways. They offer support, laughter, and a sense of belonging.

Whether it’s a heartfelt chat, a shared meal, or simply spending quality time together, these connections nourish our souls. So, let’s make a conscious effort to express gratitude for the people who make our lives brighter. A simple ‘thank you’ or a heartfelt compliment can go a long way in strengthening these bonds. After all, it's the people who truly matter.

In addition to this, I have a stash of empty 'Thank You' cards and envelopes. When the lady at the end of our avenue alerted us to the fire at 4am that day, by 8:30am I had a bunch of flowers and a thank you card on her doorstep. Then later in the week, I gave her a jar of honey. These were tiny gestures compared to her quick thinking and potential life-saving actions but they will mean a great deal to her.

It's okay to step outside your comfort zone. Every new person you meet is a potential friend. So, put on your 'best self' and start discovering new connections.

Cherishing your partner

You may already be in a long-term relationship when you reach retirement age. And that relationship might be very strong and a true 'partnership'. If that's the case then I take my hat off to you and congratulate you. But we all know that we have to work at the relationship with our partner. If we want the final years with our partner to be fun, trusting, rewarding and enjoyable, it will require resilience and effort.

You may be in a relationship that has become just a little jaded. Perhaps the spark has dimmed a little. Or maybe you've simply drifted apart over the years. Or perhaps you've both become set in your ways, predictable, stale and lacking in fun. Whatever the reason, it's never too late to reignite the flame.

Things to avoid with your partner

Therapist Jean-Claude Chalmet wrote a piece for The Times dated 24th August 2024, in which he gave nine areas that undermine marriages. After working with couples for 30 years, these are the things he believes we should all watch out for. And I think it's fair to say, most of us will be guilty of one or more of these if we have been married or living with someone for a long time.

Physical touch often reduces when couples don't feel secure. This can lead to a downward spiral of avoidance and misunderstanding. But it's important to remember that it's never too late to reconnect. Even if you feel hesitant, expressing your desire for closeness can be a powerful first step. A simple gesture, like reaching out for a hug or holding hands, can break the ice and open the door for deeper communication. Remember, vulnerability is a sign of strength, not weakness. By taking the initiative and expressing your needs, you're showing your partner that you value the connection and are willing to work on it together. It may feel risky, but the rewards can be immense.

Criticism can be a real relationship killer. It's not about giving feedback; it's about expressing disapproval in a hurtful way. Nagging criticism, especially when it's not about solving a problem, can be downright cruel. Constructive criticism is a myth. What we often think is constructive is actually a reflection of our own insecurities. When we criticise others, we're often trying to feel better about ourselves. Try recording your partner's critical moments. You might be surprised by how harsh they can be. Playing it back can be eye-opening. Ask them, "Is this really what you meant to say?" Many of these behaviours are learned in childhood. Breaking them can be tough, but it's worth it. By being aware of your own critical tendencies, you can work towards a healthier, more loving relationship.

The silent treatment and stonewalling are toxic habits that can seriously damage a relationship. Instead of avoiding conflict, they create a cold and distant atmosphere. If you're struggling with these behaviours, it's important to address them directly and honestly. If you're the one giving the silent treatment, remember that it's not a healthy way to deal with anger. It's better to communicate your feelings openly and respectfully. If you're the one receiving the silent treatment, don't let it go unaddressed. Talk to your partner calmly and express your concerns. Communication is key to a healthy relationship. By addressing these issues head-on, you can create a more open and understanding environment for both of you.

Belittling your partner is a form of bullying that can seriously damage a relationship. If you're struggling with this, it's important to address it directly. Instead of shaming or blaming, try calmly expressing how their behaviour makes you feel. This can help them become aware of their actions and open up a conversation about why they might be behaving this way. Also, it's often a learned behaviour, and by understanding its roots, you can work together to change it. Open communication is key to rebuilding trust and emotional safety in your relationship.

Contempt is one of the most destructive forces in a relationship. It's a subtle form of disrespect that can erode trust and love over time. Signs of contempt include sarcasm, mocking, and eye-rolling. When one partner consistently treats the other with contempt, it can make the other feel worthless and unheard. If you recognise yourself in this description, it's important to take action. Contempt is often a mask for underlying feelings of hurt or resentment. By understanding the root causes of your behaviour, you can work to change it. It's also crucial to have open and honest communication with your partner. Discuss how your behaviour is affecting them and be willing to listen to their perspective. With effort and commitment, it's possible to overcome contempt and rebuild a stronger relationship.

Lack of trust. Many couples struggle with trust issues, often leading to emotional withdrawal or passive-aggressive behaviour. It's important to address these issues openly and honestly. Instead of assuming negative intentions, try giving your partner the benefit of the doubt. By expressing your feelings and starting from a place of understanding, you can rebuild trust and create a healthier relationship.

Lack of appreciation is often cited by couples as a problem area. It's easy to focus on what our partners don't do. But have you considered what they do contribute? Sometimes, love is shown through practical actions, like providing for the family. Showing gratitude can make a world of difference. It's like a warm hug on a cold day. When we feel appreciated, we're more likely to go the extra mile. A little appreciation can go a long way in keeping the love alive.

Communication is an issue for many couples. They expect their partners to mind-read, avoid arguments, or avoid expressing themselves honestly. This can lead to a breakdown in their relationship. It's important to remember that you have the right to express your feelings, as long as you do so respectfully. Don't be afraid to share your thoughts and emotions, even if it might be difficult. By being honest and vulnerable, you create an opportunity for your partner to show you they care. Instead of reacting defensively, they can respond with empathy and understanding. This can help to break down barriers and strengthen your relationship.

Not accepting blame, blaming others and refusing to apologise creates serious rifts in relationships. It's important to be able to admit when you're wrong. If you or your partner struggle with this, it's crucial to address it. Instead of demanding an immediate apology, try a gentler approach. Ask your partner if they're willing to take responsibility for any part of the situation. Give them time to reflect and consider their role. Saying you are sorry isn't about admitting defeat; it's about showing respect for your partner and valuing the relationship. By taking responsibility, you can help heal wounds and strengthen your bond.

I have genuinely included these nine tips because they resonate so much with me personally. I can see that, at different times, I have been guilty of pretty much all of them. I am sure my long-suffering wife would agree. I don't consider myself to be a bad person or neglectful husband, it's just 'conditioning' over many years. A minor transgression that becomes acceptable one day can become a large irritation if it continues for any length of time. And the longer it goes on, the more ingrained it becomes and simply becomes the norm.

And now, having spoken to things to avoid, let's turn our minds more positively and think of things that we might like to do to keep our relationships fresh.

Things to consider starting with your partner when you are over 60

It's easy for relationships to fall into a comfortable rut, especially after years together. But just because you've been partners for a long time doesn't mean the fun has to stop. There are plenty of ways to keep your relationship fresh and exciting, even as you age.

Try something new: Whether it's taking a cooking class, learning to dance, or exploring a new hobby together, trying something new can reignite the spark in your relationship. It's a great way to bond over shared experiences and discover new interests.

Rediscover your shared interests: Think back to the things you enjoyed doing together when you first met. Have you drifted apart from those activities? Revisit old hobbies or explore new ones together.

Plan regular date nights: Just because you're married or in a long-term relationship doesn't mean you should stop dating. Schedule regular date nights, whether it's a fancy dinner, a movie night at home, or a weekend getaway.

Communicate openly and honestly: Regular communication is essential for maintaining a healthy relationship, even in later life. Make time to talk about your feelings, your hopes, and your dreams.

Volunteer together: Giving back to your community can be a rewarding way to spend time together and strengthen your bond.

Travel: Exploring new places together can be a great way to create lasting memories and keep your relationship exciting.

Be supportive and encouraging: Offer your partner emotional support and encouragement, especially during challenging times. Celebrate their successes and be there for them when they need you.

Keep learning and growing: Never stop learning and growing as individuals. This can help you stay connected and avoid feeling stagnant in your relationship.

In the case of my wife and I, we both love growing things in our garden. Often, we will work in the garden together, once I have set her up with a safe space and easy access for her wheelchair. And

I stay within calling distance, just in case she needs help with anything.

We also visit gardens together, things like the Royal Horticultural Gardens, one of which we are lucky to have in our home town of Harrogate. There is always easy access for the wheelchair in gardens that are open to the public. And there is usually somewhere for us to stop for coffee or lunch.

Finding love later in life

Having now covered off ideas on how to re-ignite your relationship with your partner, we turn to all of you who do not have a partner currently.

You may have lost your partner by the time you reach 60 plus. And you may have given up hope of ever meeting anyone 'special' again. You may not have fully retired and chosen instead to bury yourself in your work, trying to ignore the loneliness when everything goes quiet on an evening and you are sitting alone. You may have retired and have a comfortable life that you would love to share with someone.

Love knows no age. This adage rings especially true as we enter the vibrant chapter of life after 60 in the UK. Retirement, newfound freedom, and a desire for connection can all fuel a renewed yearning for love and companionship. But navigating the dating scene in your golden years can seem daunting. Here, we'll explore the unique landscape of finding love at 60 plus in the UK, offering tips and resources to help you on your journey.

Primary importance

The number one thing to remember is mindset. Most of us judge ourselves negatively. We go through thoughts like, "Nobody will love me", "I'm not good enough", "I'm too fat, too skinny, too tall, too short..."

I have also seen people sabotage themselves when it comes to attracting a mate. They are alone and lonely, yet they eat "comfort food" for solace from the bombardment of their own mind. They know this makes them less attractive (to the majority of people) but it's a vicious downward spiral.

When we phrase our internal dialogue like, "I hope I find the right person soon", "I need to find a steady partner" or "I can't find anyone to love me", it all comes from a place of lack. That dialogue simply endorses the fact that you do not have a partner.

Some alternate phrases might be, "I know I am loveable and loving", "I have everything in place and I can share my abundance", "I am passionate, willing and able to give love".

It's worth reminding ourselves of my recurring theme – what we think about we bring about. When we continue to live in a negative mindset, we continue to draw negativity towards us. We have to change our internal dialogue and love ourselves before we start thinking of loving someone else.

Embracing the shift:

Life after 60 often brings a beautiful shift in perspective. Children have usually grown up and left home, careers might have reached a fulfilling conclusion, and there's a newfound appreciation for time and experiences. This freedom allows space for personal growth and the pursuit of new passions, including love.

What has changed?:

The dating landscape has evolved significantly in recent years. Online dating platforms catering specifically to seniors are on the rise, offering a safe and convenient way to connect with like-minded individuals. Gone are the days of limited options – today, seniors in the UK have a wealth of resources at their fingertips.

Finding love after 60 can be a rewarding and fulfilling experience. There are many ways to meet new people and potentially find a special someone, in addition to online dating.

One option is to join social clubs or groups based on your interests. Whether you're into dancing, gardening, or book clubs, there's likely a group out there for you. These groups provide a great opportunity to meet people who share your passions.

Volunteering is another excellent way to meet new people and make a difference in your community. There are countless volunteer opportunities available, from helping at a local food bank to working with animals.

Attending events and social gatherings can also help you expand your social circle. This could include concerts, festivals, or even community events. Don't forget about your existing social network. Your friends and family might know someone who would be a good match for you.

Finding love at our age takes patience and persistence. Keep an open mind, be yourself, and enjoy the process.

Understanding your desires:

Before diving headfirst into the dating world, it's crucial to reflect on your own desires. Are you seeking a casual companion for shared activities, a travel buddy, or something deeper? Honesty with yourself will help you tailor your approach and identify potential partners who align with your goals.

The benefits of love after 60:

Studies have shown that companionship after 60 offers a plethora of benefits. It can boost mental and emotional well-being, reduce loneliness, and even contribute to a healthier lifestyle through shared activities. Love in your golden years can be a source of joy, support, and an exciting new chapter in your life.

Overcoming challenges:

Dating after 60 comes with its own set of challenges. You might encounter individuals with baggage from previous relationships, concerns about finances, or anxieties about navigating online platforms. However, these challenges can be overcome with a positive attitude, clear communication, and a willingness to explore new experiences.

Where to look:

There's no one-size-fits-all approach to finding love later in life. The UK offers a diverse range of options:

Numerous online dating platforms cater specifically to mature audiences. Sites like "OurTime," "Saga Dating," and "SilverSingles" prioritise user safety and facilitate connections based on shared interests and values.

Classic FM Radio station has its own unique website – "Dating for music lovers". There will be other 'category' sites for people with specific interests and hobbies. I highlight this one because I listen to Classic FM myself. I think it would be a wonderful idea to meet someone with whom you already have something in common.

Joining social groups focused on hobbies, activities, or interests is a fantastic way to meet like-minded individuals. Local walking groups, art classes, or book clubs can be fertile ground for sparking connections.

The UK hosts a range of senior-friendly events and activities, from singles dances to cultural outings. Participating in these events exposes you to new people and offers conversation starters.

Don't underestimate the power of your existing network! This is a reminder to let your friends and family know you're open to meeting someone new.

Another thing to remember is to ‘shine your light’ so that people who meet you for the first time will see that you are available and open to approach. You know when a London black cab is available don’t you? They have their yellow light on top of the cab glowing brightly. Make sure this is you! Put on a bright appearance, respond to people with a smile and with kindness.

Making the most of the experience

Here are some tips to enhance your dating experience after 60:

Embrace your life experiences and the wisdom you've acquired. Be confident - confidence is an attractive quality at any age.

Honesty and clear communication are paramount in any relationship. Be upfront about your expectations and desires.

Don't rush into anything. Getting to know someone takes time. Enjoy the process of getting acquainted and exploring your compatibility.

Listen to your intuition. If something feels off, it probably is. Don't be afraid to walk away from a situation that doesn't resonate with you.

Be open to trying new things and exploring activities you might not have considered before. This can lead to unexpected connections.

Dating safety tips:

Always meet for your first date in a well-lit public place and let someone know where you're going and who you're meeting.

Don't rush into intimacy or financial commitments. Take your time to build trust and get to know the person better.

Do not lend your new connection any money. We are all more vulnerable in these situations and there are some that will try to take advantage of us.

If someone makes you feel uncomfortable or pressured, stop right there. Trust your instincts.

Be cautious about sharing personal information online or on first dates.

Additional resources:

Age UK

This leading UK charity offers support and guidance for seniors, including resources on relationships and finding companionship. (www.ageuk.org.uk/information-advice/health-wellbeing/relationships-family/)

Digital matchmaking for seniors

When searching on the above words, first on the list was top10datingsites.co.uk. There I found a 'Top Three' selection. Comments are provided by www.top10datingsites.co.uk

OurTime: One of the best dating sites for women and men over 50. This dating service can be used for singles over 50 looking to find other singles over 50, or by someone younger seeking a mature partner with more life experience and wisdom to share.

eharmony: The #1 trusted dating app for serious relationships. Signup takes 3 steps: Profile Set Up, Match Preferences, and Compatibility Quiz. eharmony is not only one of the most popular online dating apps, but it's also one of the most affordable websites with 6-, 12-, or 24-month plans for as low as $6.97/month.

Match.com: Recognised as one of the more "serious" dating websites you use when you're ready to settle down. Pricing is a bit expensive with Standard or Premium plans ranging up to $36.99/month for 3 months or 1 full month for $62.65. As a fully subscribed member, you can email and chat with people, check profile visitors, get an annual profile review, receive monthly boosts, and attend in-person Match Events.

Summary

There are many reasons why we need to take care and nurture our relationships as we reach maturity. Our friends and relatives are becoming fewer, so the people we have left are more important to us.

We may have retired and have no day job, perhaps leaving us to wonder what to do with ourselves each day. We need to dust ourselves off and get out into society.

People who have strong social connections tend to be happier and healthier.

As we become more mature, we become more vulnerable to loneliness and social isolation – and it can have a serious effect on the health of the elderly. We have covered different ways to overcome loneliness, even if you live alone and find it hard to get out.

You might be living alone and have decided to carry on working through what should have been your retirement – because there is not much interest in being on your own in your house all day.

Retirement can also bring about a sense of isolation, as we may find ourselves with more time on our hands than we know what to do with.

It's essential to stay connected with others and actively seek out social opportunities. Whether it's joining a club, volunteering, or simply spending time with loved ones, having strong social connections can significantly improve our well-being.

Loneliness can be a serious health risk for older adults, leading to both physical and mental health problems.

For those who find themselves alone, there are many options available. Consider moving to a retirement community, joining a senior centre, or using online platforms to connect with others. It's never too late to make new friends.

If you're looking for a romantic partner, there are plenty of opportunities. Online dating, social events, and even volunteering can be great ways to meet new people.

Then, of course, there are those of us who have reached retirement and we are still living with our husband or wife or partner. It’s important that we cherish the love we have today and lift it to new heights. We’ve gone through some of the things that we need to stop doing with our partners because they will be having a negative effect on the relationship. And we covered some of the things we might want to start doing, to add extra interest to our final years together.

Ultimately, the key to fulfilling relationships is mindset. What we think about, we bring about. If we focus on positivity, love, and connection, we're more likely to attract those qualities into our lives. Let’s be big and bold as possible. You can make your final years full of joy, friendship and love – just do it!

Nurturing our connections is vital and so is ensuring our security. A strong support network is invaluable, and so is a stable financial foundation.

Strong relationships often involve shared experiences and mutual support. But sometimes, support also means navigating the practical aspects of life together, including finances.

So, let's move directly on to the next chapter for help and guidance on how we might live our 'golden years' in financial comfort.

Chapter 5 – Handling finances

"The greatest wealth is to live content with what one has."

Plato

We need to talk about money, honey! So please forgive me if some of this becomes a little heavy. Taking care of finances should be a fun adventure, so I will try to stay light!

Once we've reached 60 we probably have a different perspective on finances and usually, we have different priorities. We are going to start by looking at some fundamentals we all need to take care of and then we are going to discuss ways in which we can improve our financial situation by improving our wealth.

Everything we will speak of in this chapter assumes you are reading this at around age 60 or over. I know there will be readers who are a number of years off that age too and this will help you start financial planning earlier, which will give you a greater chance of a positive outcome. The sooner you start, the more secure will be your financial future.

Subjects in this chapter:

- Plan for the future
- Reduce cost and optimise savings
- Create wealth

As in all the things we are discussing together in this guide, finance is not meant to give you something to stress over! Treat money as a 'tool' that will help you achieve a happier and more secure final quarter of your life. Money itself will not lead to happiness or longevity. It is simply part of a bigger picture. Please do not let this chapter make you become 'hung up' on your finances. It's just that I realise that it is important to a lot of people and so it needs to be included in our wholistic view of becoming 60.

In addition, I would like us all to be spared the dreaded statement, "I can't afford that!" and empower all 60 plus people to change their thinking and say instead, "what do I need to do, to be able to afford that?"

Planning future finances

We need to prepare for a comfortable life expectancy of more than 20 years after our sixtieth birthday. Of course, this will need a personalised approach, as needs and situations vary. However, here is some general guidance to help you get started:

Assess your current financial situation:

Income: Lots of sixty year olds will be approaching retirement. This means those of you working in countries where there is a state pension will be looking at the date when this becomes available. At the time of writing the retirement age in UK, USA and Australia is 66. Interestingly, the age in India is between 58 and 60. We can all continue to work beyond this age if we wish to, so for the sake of this exercise we are just assessing the income we can truly forecast.

Income can also be received from a pension you might have with your employer. In this arrangement, your employer contributes toward your pension and you contribute a slightly lesser amount. In my case, I was no longer working with the employer that I began the pension scheme with, so at age 50 I was able to take my company pension early. This made sense, because neither party was contributing to the fund, so the money was just sitting inactive.

You may have also added to your pension by taking out a private pension fund, where only you have been making contributions.

Further sources of income might be from the interest earned on savings accounts, term deposits, bonds or other fixed-income investments. You should also be able to assess the dividend income from any shares you own. And, if you are lucky, you may have net capital gains from any investment sales.

Expenses: write down your monthly expenses across categories like housing, food, healthcare, transportation, leisure and debt payments. These categories can be further sub-divided into things like groceries, dining out, utilities, etc. You can use budgeting apps, a spreadsheet or plain old pencil and paper, to track your weekly spend.

Look to see if any expenses can be reduced or optimised. Put your expenses into categories like 'essential' and 'discretionary' and see if anything can be reduced or replaced with a lower cost alternative. Contact service providers like phone, broadband, cable companies to explore alternatives. Cancel recurring subscriptions that you no longer need. Planning your meals and grocery shopping with a list can help avoid impulse purchases and food waste, reducing grocery spending.

Regularly review your spending and look for opportunities to further optimise. Set small, achievable goals for reducing specific expenses and track your progress.

Improve expenses by looking at credit cards or loyalty programs that offer cash back or rewards on your purchases, maximising your return on spending. Take advantage of discounts: Look for coupons, promo codes, and discounts before making purchases, especially online. For frequently used items, consider buying in bulk if it brings cost savings but be mindful of overspending or spoilage. Renegotiate loans: Explore refinancing existing loans with lower interest rates, potentially reducing your monthly payments.

Pay off any high-interest debt before retirement to reduce your financial burden.

Assets and debts: Savings includes readily available cash in bank accounts, emergency funds, and short-term savings goals. Think of it as a safety net and a source for immediate needs. Investments like long-term holdings like stocks, bonds, mutual funds, or real estate that aim to grow your wealth over time. They generate income through dividends, interest, or potential appreciation. Include your home, rental properties, or any other land or buildings you own. Owning property can provide income, appreciation, and a sense of security.

Then look at liabilities like mortgages, which are loans taken out to purchase a property, with the property itself acting as collateral. Mortgage payments typically have a fixed interest rate and repayment schedule. Personal loans, student loans (I know, we are addressing over 60s and I'm writing about student loans – but it's possible!), car loans, etc., fall under this category. They have varying interest rates and repayment terms and can significantly impact your cash flow. Credit card debt can quickly spiral out of control. Prioritising paying off this debt is crucial for financial health.

Speaking of "health" - consider potential future healthcare needs and long-term care costs, factoring in existing conditions and family history. Prioritise regular check-ups and preventive care to maintain your health and reduce the risk of chronic diseases.

Set a budget: prioritise essential expenses and ensure your budget covers housing, food, utilities, and essential healthcare. Allocate for discretionary spending and include reasonable amounts for activities, travel, hobbies, and gifts. Factor in inflation by assuming there will be rising costs of living over 20 years. Review and adjust regularly by updating your budget as income, expenses, and priorities change.

Optimise your savings and investments:

Assuming you are still working, you will be able to contribute as much as you can toward pensions and retirement accounts. Take advice on how you can use tax-advantaged methods that are relevant to your home country. They will be things like IRAs or 401(k)s in the USA, your works pension fund in the UK, Superannuation and Pension Funds in Australia and so on.

Diversify your portfolio into their risk category. Low-risk investments for income are your reliable performers, generating consistent income in the form of dividends or interest. Think bonds, Certificate of Deposit, or income-focused funds. While their growth potential is modest, they act as anchors, providing stability during market downturns. Higher-risk investments for growth are the adrenaline rush of the portfolio, offering the potential for significant capital appreciation, especially in the long run. Stocks, real estate, or growth-oriented funds fall under this category. However, they also come with increased volatility, meaning their value can fluctuate more dramatically.

The key lies in finding the right mix for your risk tolerance and financial goals. If you are approaching 60 with a few years to go, you might favour a higher allocation to growth assets, while someone who is already at retirement might prioritise income-generating investments for stability.

The closer you are to retirement, the less time you have to recover from potential losses. Therefore, a higher allocation to low-risk investments might be prudent. Your risk tolerance will need to be considered. How comfortable are you with market volatility? If the sight of fluctuating prices gives you heartburn, focus on a more conservative portfolio. Consider your financial goals. Are you saving for a specific goal, like a down payment, or aiming for long-term wealth accumulation? Align your risk profile with your goals.

Rebalance your portfolio periodically: Adjust your asset allocation based on market changes and your risk tolerance.

Seek professional advice: Consult a financial advisor for personalised investment strategies. This is touched on again later, when we look at Wealth Creation.

Plan for healthcare and long-term care:

Evaluate health insurance options. Research Medical Care plans and consider supplemental insurance for gaps. Explore long-term care options: Learn about assisted living facilities, home care services, and their associated costs. Discuss your wishes with family by communicating your preferences for care and living arrangements with loved ones.

Taking proactive steps in these areas empowers you to face the future with confidence. By understanding your healthcare options, exploring long-term care possibilities, and openly communicating with loved ones, you can make informed decisions about your future well-being and ensure a comfortable and secure later life.

Planning ahead gives you greater control and avoids making hasty decisions under duress. It allows you to age with dignity and ensure your loved ones are equipped to support you according to your preferences. Start the conversation, do your research, and take control of your future healthcare and long-term care needs.

Think about where you would like to live

Where you choose to live in retirement can significantly impact your overall quality of life. Retirement living expenses can vary widely depending on location. Research different areas to find one that fits your budget. Factors to consider include housing costs, taxes, utilities, and healthcare expenses.

Being close to loved ones can provide emotional support and practical assistance. Consider the importance of family and friends in your life and how close you want to be to them.

Ensure that your chosen location has adequate healthcare facilities and services. Research hospitals, clinics, and doctors in the area. Consider factors like wait times, quality of care, and insurance coverage.

Think about your desired lifestyle. Do you prefer a bustling city, a quiet suburb, or a rural retreat? Consider factors like climate, amenities, and recreational opportunities.

Research the local community to see if it offers activities and social opportunities that align with your interests.

If you have mobility limitations, ensure your chosen location is accessible. Consider factors like transportation options, walkability, and availability of accessible housing.

Think about your future needs. Will you require assisted living or nursing home care in the future? Consider the availability of these services in your chosen location.

Now the Good News!

Forgive me, I felt that last section on planning started to become a little heavy! So, I thought a positive sub-title might lighten things up a bit. We do all need to plan but we must not lose sight of the goal, which is to find joy in our later years.

By planning proactively and adapting your approach as needed, you can significantly increase your chances of enjoying a comfortable and fulfilling life right through to your eighties and beyond.

For some, reaching 60 will mean a reduction in 'work' activities, possibly due to retirement or moving to part-time work or some other reason. This will allow those people to spend more time on focusing on their finances and may even prompt them to start thinking of wealth creation. Maybe you always wanted to look at a 'side hustle' or you have had a burning passion to start your own business or you would like an extra income but have not had the time, until now. Maybe you are already investing as a hobby and now able to spend more time doing more of it.

Now we are going to drill down more into this concept of creating wealth and look at how we can all apply this now that we are 'more mature'.

Wealth creation

I feel the need to set out what is trying to be achieved in this next section. A kind of 'trailer' for what's to follow.

You might be anywhere on the age range from early 50's to late 80's. It would be much better if you start following the suggestions here when you are younger. However, this can still achieve levels of success for you, whatever age you start. And I am trying to include those people who have reached this age and have already created some wealth for themselves and include those people who haven't.

This might sound a little strange but why would you want to create wealth? I mean, what is it for? Think about your "Why?" before you set out to make money. Make your 'Why' big and attach emotion to it. The reason is, it will help you later when things might become 'stuck,' and progress is not what you expected. When we make our reason bigger than us, it becomes more important for us to continue.

Your 'Why' could be to retire early, so that you can enjoy the latter part of your life doing exciting things with your grandchildren (even if you do not have any yet!!). It might be to allow you to put more back into your family and/or community – leave a legacy by building something that outlasts you. It might be an enabler to allow you to do something you have always dreamed of like travel the world or go back to the world of academia and study subjects you are interested in.

While wealth is not the sole measure of happiness, it can contribute to your well-being and enable you to pursue your dreams and aspirations. It might allow a better quality of life, allowing the provision of better healthcare, education, and choice of housing. Personal interests can also be pursued when you are supported financially.

What we must not do is let the process of wealth creation cause us any mental anxiety. Someone told me years ago, "If I won a million, I would just have a million things to worry about." Whilst this was never my philosophy, I did understand their sentiment.

The pursuit of wealth should be balanced with ethical considerations and a focus on our well-being. The reasons for creating wealth are deeply personal and should align with your values and life goals.

There are lots of ways we can go about creating wealth. If you are already on a journey of wealth creation, there will something here to help you on your way. Here are ten steps you can follow to ensure success.

1. Define success: Aim beyond your needs in your financial goal. I always asked my two children to "aim for the stars, so that if you reach the moon, you will have achieved something awesome." In the same vein, I have always set a 'stretch' target. Not to beat yourself up about if you do not reach it. No, it is because you never know what you are capable of until you try.

I am not a track and field athlete. But I am sure when they run a distance race they are thinking about the area beyond the white tape at the end. They would not want to simply aim for the tape and slow down as they get close.

Visualise where you want to be and what you want to achieve. This is important. See your ambition achieved and feel the emotion as if you were already living with that success. This is once again reminding you that your internal dialogue and your emotions will determine ALL of your success.

A well-defined concept of success means you can measure your progress accurately. You can track how far you have come and adjust if necessary to stay on the right path. It will also ensure that your pursuit of wealth aligns with your personal values and principles. This prevents you from compromising your ethics or sacrificing other important aspects of your life for the sake of financial gain.

Success is subjective, and what it means to you may differ from others – so define your own success and tailor your wealth-building strategies to your unique desires and circumstances. Financial success can contribute to emotional well-being, but it is important to understand how much wealth is necessary for your happiness. A defined success metric helps you strike a balance between wealth and well-being.

2. Develop a budget: If you are approaching the age of 60, you will most likely be in a job. And, like most people, you probably live to the level of your earnings – meaning you spend everything you earn! Here in this step, I am asking you to stop and think. Track spending patterns and identify areas where you do not need to be spending and some ideas are provided earlier in this chapter. Getting this right will instil a discipline in you that will foster mindful spending. It is important so that you set off on your path of controlled financial growth and the level of prosperity you have selected for yourself.

You might need to lower your outgoings or increase your income to be able to build wealth. Create a household budget that allows headroom between what you earn and what you spend.

As suggested above, another way to create headroom between income and spending is to raise your income. Again, if you are approaching 60 or have reached the golden age already, you are most likely to be employed. When going to your manager to ask for a raise, be sure you can elucidate the value you bring to your job. They will not pay more for 'more of the same' - so spell it out for them. You could move jobs for one with better pay. Better still, you could get a job offer that is higher paid and show the offer to your manager. You either receive an uplift in pay or take the other job.

If you are buying something large, see if you can get interest-free payment terms and spread the cost over time. Of course, you will need to have a sound credit rating and there are several ways you can check that.

Overall, having a budget should provide you with discipline and peace of mind.

3. Save and invest: Now that you are managing to retain some of your earnings, you will be able to start saving. Saving is the foundation, allowing you to accumulate a safety net for emergencies and unexpected expenses. It cultivates the discipline needed to live within your means and directs a portion of your income toward achieving your goals. Investing, on the other hand, takes your financial journey a step further. It involves strategically deploying your saved funds into assets that have the potential to grow over time, generating returns that outpace inflation.

Saving and investing are the dynamic duo that will help you create wealth. Saving gives you a secure foundation and helps shield you from 'rainy days'. While investing accelerates your financial growth through compound interest.

This is always a balancing act. Your aim is to achieve your financial goal and have the peace of mind that your money is working as hard as you are.

Start early and make sure you are consistent. Embrace the power of saving and investing and you will be far more confident to hit your 'stretch' target. And importantly, you will be in a better position to take advantage of entrepreneurial opportunities when they come along – more on this later.

4. Diversify your investments: There are many ways to invest your savings and your choices will also need to consider your feelings about each one's 'risk factor.' Usually, the lower the risk the lower the return, i.e., less interest paid.

One route would be to save until you have enough to justify moving some money from your savings account to an investment product, to gain a better interest. Not the whole amount of the savings, just the amount you feel comfortable in investing. Perhaps using example figures might help explain it better.

You might feel you need to keep 1,000 in case of emergencies. So, you wait until you have saved 2,000 and invest only the amount above your emergency figure and put 1,000 into an investment product. The next time you have 2,000 saved you would move 1,000 again but into a different investment product. These numbers are simply to show the principle. Only you will have an idea what an emergency figure might be and that will depend on your circumstances. In my case, I raised it when the children were born.

The types of investments you choose will also depend on how much time you have to research the market. One way to short-circuit investment research is to find a financial advisor. They will take a fee in some form or another but they should be able to justify their fee by the better advice they provide and the higher returns you receive.

Another way might be for you to use Tracker funds and ETFs. These are passive investments that follow a market index, offering low fees, diversification, and long-term growth potential. While ETFs trade like stocks for flexibility, both options provide a simple, cost-effective way to invest without actively picking stocks.

You will wish to reduce the impact of inferior performance in any single investment on your overall portfolio. Different assets tend to react differently to market fluctuations, economic changes, and geopolitical events. When one asset class experiences a downturn, another might thrive, helping balance out losses.

Different investments behave like different ingredients in your financial recipe. Some might shine while others are having a quiet day. By spreading your money across assorted options – like stocks, bonds, real estate, and perhaps a sprinkle of cryptocurrencies – you are not putting all your eggs in one basket. If one part is not doing so well, your other investments can pick up the slack and keep your portfolio balanced.

Diversification also helps align your portfolio with your risk tolerance and financial goals. If you are risk-averse, you can allocate a larger portion to more stable assets, while still having exposure to higher-risk, higher-reward options if you are comfortable with it.

Also consider the ethics of each fund you choose. We all have our own view of what we will and will not tolerate in terms of ethical investment. I personally would not wish to benefit from investments into funds that might cause misery and suffering to other souls – human or non-human.

5. Continuous learning: Leading on directly from diversification, the more time you allocate to managing your own savings and investments, the more you will enjoy the journey. And continuous learning becomes your superpower.

I would recommend everyone read "Simple Wealth, Inevitable Wealth" by Nick Murray. The author is a financial advisor – so he advises we employ someone like him. Well, he would say that wouldn't he? However, we can still take the messages in his book and do very well investing on our own.

Imagine you are in a game where the rules keep evolving. If you are not learning, you might get left behind. But when you stay curious and keep educating yourself about money matters, investing, and business trends, you are like a Jedi – ready to tackle any challenge.

Learning keeps your brain buzzing and your ideas fresh. It helps you adapt to new situations, seize opportunities, and even bounce back from setbacks. The more you know, the better decisions you can make. Plus, knowledge is your secret weapon when it comes to smart investments and spotting the next important thing.

So, whether you are reading books, taking online courses, or just keeping an ear out for innovative ideas, remember that learning is not a one-time thing. It is a lifelong adventure that keeps your mind sharp, your strategies on point, and your wealth-building journey exciting. Stay curious – the more you learn, the more you can earn!

When you feel you are starting to understand the investment world, you might start looking at investing directly in companies on the stock market. At that point, you will need to know how to analyse a business to understand it's fundamental value. This is the big boy's world and you need time to study.

6. Join an investment club: One way to short-circuit your learning is to join an investment club, preferably in your local area, so that you can meet face to face. Investment clubs can help people learn and discuss potential investment strategies as well as their goals. Some investment clubs pool their money, which can help people be a part of a cohesive investing strategy. They will all be individuals like you, and all have their strengths to bring to the group.

The following information on investment clubs was gleaned from the Motley Fool website – www.fool.co.uk:

Clubs occasionally seek new members to replace those who have moved away or left for other reasons and they may try and invite new members to join. However, this tends to be an infrequent occurrence so it can be hard to find the right club that's also looking for a new member.

Members of such clubs probably already have some friends they plan to invite. Your best bet might be to ask people you know whether they are in an investment club and whether they are looking for new members.

You might expect that if a club's account has grown over many years and its average member's stake is in the thousands of pounds that a new joiner would be expected to contribute a huge sum of money in order to join. That's not true, though, as the accounting methods that most clubs use permit new members to begin by just contributing the standard monthly amount. Longer-term members will each retain bigger pieces of the pie, and everyone's piece is calculated according to how much was contributed when.

If you find that there are no local clubs open to new members, you can start your own. Three key roles are the Chair, who runs the meetings, the Treasurer, who looks after the financial aspects and keeps the records, and the Secretary, who keeps records of what's discussed and decided in each meeting. It's a good idea to shift these roles around, perhaps changing who does them each year.

You should decide how many people you want to involve and how new members will be accepted. You also need to decide how much money to put in, how frequently, and whether everyone puts in the same amount. You'll need to decide a name for your club as well. Setting up a preliminary meeting to discuss topics like this is often the best approach and makes sure everyone is in agreement before you get started investing.

Of course, you'll probably want to tweak how things are run as you go, when you learn what works and what doesn't, but having a basic framework that everyone has signed up to can keep everything running more smoothly and efficiently.

You could even join an online investment club if you would prefer. You would lose a lot of the fun of sharing ideas with like-minded people and having a group with whom you could share your success.

As with many things, what you get from an investment club will depend in large part by the effort you put into it. It's a great way to learn about investing or perhaps experiment with a slightly different style of investing that you don't normally use with your other investments.

7. Control yourself!: I say this tongue in cheek but it is true. We are all easily swayed by outside forces when we are on our wealth creation journey. When you control yourself, you're making mindful decisions about spending and saving. It is not about saying "no" to everything fun but about saying "yes" to your bigger dreams. Saving money today means you will have the resources to chase after those awesome adventures, investments, and experiences in the future.

We start to build our small nest-egg. A temptation comes our way to buy something. Our resolution goes out of the window and before we know it, we have some latest gadget that eventually ends up in a cupboard.

One of the most fundamental things to learn is to keep up the discipline of investing every month. This is the rule of 'pound (or dollar) cost averaging.' Prices of investments vary month on month. When the market is up, your investment fund will buy you fewer shares and when the market is down, you receive more shares. By maintaining this year after year, you even out market fluctuations and just see the overall improvement.

But this takes enormous strength of will. If you feel you might struggle with this, then get guidance from a financial advisor and pay him what he is due. He will help you keep the faith as the markets are in turmoil around you. Which they will be - because you are in this for the long haul.

Remember, every penny you don't spend on an impulse buy is a penny that could be growing in your investment pot. Self-control might mean passing up that instant gratification, but it's your key to long-term financial satisfaction.

Avoid impulsive spending and focus on long-term gains by monthly increments.

8. Manage debt responsibly: Keep your debt in check. Be careful with credit card purchases. When you are managing the "Savings and Investment" element correctly, you will be able to take advantage of paying off credit card bills every month, without incurring a fee. Responsible debt management means using it strategically – taking on debt for things that have the potential to grow your wealth, like education or a well-thought-out business idea.

Managing debt is important for achieving long-term goals. Prioritise high-interest debts and pay them off first. You might find debt consolidation a useful way to help lower the interest rate or simplify your payments.

Communicate with the people or organisations to whom you owe money if you start to face repayment problems. Managing debt properly allows you to build back a positive credit history and reduce your stress.

Imagine debt as a friendly dragon – it can be tamed and even become your ally. When you manage it wisely, you are giving yourself the freedom to fly towards financial success. But here's the catch: you have got to keep that dragon in check. High-interest debts can breathe fire on your financial dreams.

9. Passive income: Continuing with this fairy-tale imagery – imagine passive income as your financial Harry Potter, casting his spells behind the scenes to make your money grow while you focus on other stuff. Active income is like trading time for money – you work, you get paid. But passive income is like the magic wand that gives time back to you.

Passive income sources, like rental properties, investments, or royalties from creative work, provide an income that does not require a great deal of your attention. Granted, they often require a lot of effort upfront – setting up, investing, or creating – but then they keep working for you.

Think of it as your ticket to freedom. With passive income, you are not tied to a 9-to-5 grind forever. It gives you flexibility to pursue your passions, travel, or just enjoy more leisure time. Alternatively, you could use the lessons learned and simply re-invest your passive income.

Passive income builds your empire. It is like planting seeds that grow into money trees. The more you nurture them, the more they bear fruit. And that fruit? It is financial freedom and a wealthier, worry-free future. So, wave that magic wand and start creating those passive income streams – your future self will thank you!

The types of passive income vary and will depend on your own style. It could be renting out property, owning stocks that pay dividends, creating an online course or authoring a book. You might start affiliate marketing, blogging, sell stock photos you have taken or start a drop shipping online store. This latter idea and many other income producing ideas are well covered in "The 4-Hour Work Week" by Tim Ferris and if you are considering starting a micro business to generate passive income, I recommend you read Tim's book.

Here are some more 'in-depth' thoughts on the types of passive income you might wish to create and you are able to mix and match them. This next section, on investing money, assumes you have money to start with. If that is not you, then simply put a 'post it' note on this page and return to it when you have generated spare cash from some of the ideas in the next chapter, where we discover ways to earn extra income.

Low-Risk investments

If you're looking for a safe and stable investment option, consider these low-risk strategies:

Savings Accounts: While savings accounts typically offer lower interest rates than other investment options, they provide a secure place to store your money. Look for high-yield savings accounts to maximise your returns.

Cash ISAs (Individual Savings Accounts): In the UK, Cash ISAs offer tax-free savings. They are a great way to save for specific goals like a house deposit or retirement.

Government Bonds: Government bonds are generally considered low-risk investments as they are backed by the government. They offer a fixed interest rate and are a good option for those seeking stability.

Medium-Risk investments

For a balance of risk and reward, consider these medium-risk options:

Index Funds: These funds track a specific market index, such as the FTSE 100 or S&P 500. They offer diversification and lower fees compared to actively managed funds.

Corporate Bonds: Corporate bonds are issued by companies to raise capital. They offer higher interest rates than government bonds but carry slightly higher risk.

Dividend-Paying Stocks: Investing in companies that pay regular dividends can provide a steady income stream. However, it's important to research individual companies and their financial health.

High-Risk investments

If you're willing to take on more risk for potentially higher returns, consider these high-risk options:

Individual Stocks: Investing in individual stocks can offer significant returns, but it also carries higher risk. Research companies carefully before investing and diversify your portfolio to manage risk.

In the USA, you might try investing in real estate, such as rental properties or real estate investment trusts (REITs), which can offer potential returns but also involves significant risks.

Venture Capital: Investing in early-stage companies can offer high returns but also carries high risk. This is suitable for investors with a high-risk tolerance and a long-term investment horizon.

Cryptocurrencies: Investing in cryptocurrencies like Bitcoin or Ethereum can offer significant returns, but it's also highly volatile and speculative. Do your research and understand the risks before investing in cryptocurrencies.

Angel investing or venture capital: Fund early-stage businesses with high growth potential, seeking significant returns upon their success. Requires significant capital and carries high risk.

Remember, passive income doesn't mean effortless income. Most options require initial effort and ongoing maintenance. Diversify your income streams to mitigate risk and ensure stability. Carefully research and understand the risks involved before investing any money.

Seek professional advice if needed, especially for complex investments.

Look back at step 7 (Control yourself) above for entrepreneurial advice and guidance. You could go full-time into this but for it to be considered passive income, it would need to be something you set up whilst you were keeping down your day job and then keeping it running when you retire.

10. Be patient: Creating wealth takes time. Keep working towards your goals. Think of it like growing flowers in a garden – you plant seeds, water them, and wait for them to bloom. Wealth creation works in a similar way. It's easy to want instant results, but being patient means you are in it for the long haul. You are not swayed by short-term trends or hasty decisions.

Find someone you can share your Wealth Creation goals with. In step 6 above we covered the option to join an investment group to meet like-minded people. And in the same step we were introduced to the idea of having a Financial Advisor. Perhaps your partner or best friend could support you in your ideas. Having someone to speak to about your plans helps you to hold more of a 'big picture' view and this will go a long way to being patient.

Just like your garden needs time to bear fruit, your investments need time to grow. Compound interest, the eighth wonder of the world, works its magic when you give it time.

Three fundamental takeaways for Wealth Creation

Invest every month – pound (or dollar) cost averaging evens out the market's anomalies. When you invest consistently, you buy when prices are high and when they are low, balancing out your costs. Over time, your investments grow, and you benefit from the magic of compound interest. So, do not wait for the perfect moment – start small, invest every month, and watch your wealth flourish.

Keep learning – reading and online tutorials. Managing your own money is fun and rewarding. Keeping learning is like collecting gems of knowledge to make that treasure grow. In the world of wealth creation, things change – new strategies, tech, opportunities. By learning continuously, you are staying sharp. You adapt, make smarter decisions, and catch those golden chances others might miss. Learning about finance, investments, and business is like having a map through a complex jungle. Read books, follow online courses, watch podcasts – they are your tools to uncover the wealth waiting out there. Keep learning, keep growing, and keep creating wealth.

Keep a healthy reserve. Try not to have to sell (cash in) investments due to emergencies. Also, instead of relying on credit cards or loans, you have got your back covered. A reserve lets you stay on track, keep investing, and ride out storms without derailing your wealth creation plans. Think of it as your financial stronghold – protecting you when you need it most. Build your reserve and let your wealth journey be smooth and stress-free.

Healthcare provision

Maybe it's because this looms large in my life. Maybe it's because this is something that concerns a massive proportion of the retired and soon-to-be retired population. Maybe this is affecting you right now. Whatever it is, I just felt inclined to re-visit this before we leave this chapter. As I've explained earlier, I had to increase my earnings so that my wife and I could continue to live reasonably when her health deteriorated to the extent that we had to employ someone to look after her.

Healthcare costs can be significant, especially as we age. Evaluate your health insurance options and consider supplemental coverage to address any gaps. Research long-term care options, such as assisted living or nursing home care, and plan accordingly.

Choosing a suitable retirement residence is crucial for your overall well-being. Consider factors like cost of living, proximity to family and friends, access to healthcare, and lifestyle preferences. Research different communities and neighbourhoods to find one that aligns with your needs and desires.

Even if you remain in the same home, adjustments may need to be made, adding further costs to a stretched budget.

Summary

Try not to get too hung up on money. When we believe we are poor, that is the world we create for ourselves – and the opposite is true. Maintain a positive mindset.

We have seen how retirement is a significant milestone. With life expectancy increasing, it's reasonable to anticipate enjoying retirement for over two decades.

Financial planning is key because financial security is a cornerstone of a comfortable retirement. Start by assessing your current financial situation.

Identify areas where you can cut costs or optimise spending. Plan your meals and grocery shop with a list to avoid impulse purchases and food waste.

If you're still working, continue to contribute to your retirement savings as much as you can afford. Consider using tax-advantaged retirement accounts like 401(k)s or IRAs. In the UK, you might look at a Self-Invested Personal Pension (SIPP) or an ISA.

Here's a secret: success is subjective. Don't get bogged down by other people's definitions. Define what success means to you. Think big!

Most people spend what they earn. But to build wealth, we need to break this cycle. Track your spending patterns to identify areas where you can cut back.

You might be approaching retirement age and living comfortably on your current income. But consider this: could you save a little more?

Saving is the foundation. It creates a safety net for emergencies and unexpected expenses. It also cultivates the discipline needed to live within your means.

The more involved you are in managing your finances, the more confident and empowered you'll become. Embrace lifelong learning!

Building wealth takes time. Don't get discouraged if you don't see instant results.

So, now that we have discussed how to invest what money you might have, let's look at ways to earn new money – money you don't have yet!

Chapter 6 – Your next enterprise

"Age is no barrier. It's a limitation you put on your mind."

Jackie Joyner-Kersee

That quote is especially true when it comes to creating new opportunities, including financial ones. Let's explore how you can turn your experience and passion into an income stream.

So, you are reaching pensionable age or you are already benefitting from your pension. You are continuing to work or you have time to educate yourself and time to invest in new ideas.

In the last chapter we looked at creating wealth from the point of view of managing what you have and getting the most benefit from your income, whilst reducing your outgoings. In this chapter, we are looking at creating wealth from a completely different point of view – creating it from nothing!

Subjects in this chapter:

- Create additional income streams
- Think like an entrepreneur
- Getting started on a low budget
- New business ideas
- Embrace Artificial Intelligence (AI)

Start your own business: Explore entrepreneurial ideas to create additional income streams. This is your chance for an adventure that will challenge you and yet reward you when you get it right.

You may already be happily employed and looking for some 'side hustle' or thinking about leaving the corporate world to set up on your own. Maybe there has always something you have wanted to do and now that you are approaching retirement, it's become possible.

When you are thinking about starting your own business, here are some basic points for you to keep in mind.

Discover your passion: What is it that lights you up? When we align what we love with a business idea, our passion fuels our dedication and hard work – making it easier to handle the problems that might lie ahead. You might be doing this for a long time into the future so make sure you choose to do something you love. As I became more mature, I received far more satisfaction in helping people to achieve their success than all the previous years, where I was focused on my success. Think about how you can help others so that both giver and receiver profit and make that into your passion. **This is how the universe works – like a mirror. What we give out we receive back**.

Research your idea: What is the market potential? Who would be your target customers? Speak to potential customers to gain feedback and refine your product or service. Research helps you avoid pitfalls and surprises, making your journey smoother.

When developing an idea, misleadingly positive feedback can be a major obstacle, especially from friends and family who want to be supportive. Ask the right questions and focus on real experiences rather than seeking approval.

Explore how people have previously dealt with similar challenges. If they haven't actively sought a solution before, the issue may not be as significant as you assume. The best information comes from uncovering frustrations, workarounds, and genuine needs. The most reliable signs that your idea will work come from real commitments, such as a willingness to pre-order, introduce a contact, or schedule a follow-up meeting.

The way questions are framed directly impacts the quality of responses. Leading questions should be avoided, as they push people toward responses that confirm existing biases. Instead of asking whether a specific feature would be useful, it's better to ask how they currently manage a particular issue.

Hearing that an idea won't work may feel discouraging, but this information ultimately saves time and resources. The key to gathering meaningful insights is to focus on past behaviour, avoid biases, and seek tangible commitments rather than compliments. By doing so, it becomes easier to determine whether your idea addresses a real problem and has genuine market demand before investing too much time and effort.

Business Plan: Your roadmap to success. It should cover your mission, vision, target market, competitive analysis, financial projections, and strategies for marketing. This plan will be extremely useful it you need to attract investors or borrow money to get started. Some people will work hard at this and create a 65-page document full of detail. That is OK. But it is possible to fit all you need for a 3-year plan on a single A3 sheet. Do not burn your time writing a long-winded plan if that is what becomes your blocker to progress.

Be ready for setbacks: You need to be resilient because the entrepreneurial journey is not always smooth. You will be challenged and face uncertainties. Being resilient and maintaining a growth mindset will help you recover from mistakes and adapt to changing circumstances.

Build a strong network: Surround yourself with mentors and professionals who can offer guidance. Having a wide network will open new doors to opportunities and insights. I have spent my time self-employed since 2005 providing help for other business owners looking to either start their business or grow their business. There are some charlatans in the Business Coaching world out there but there are also some very capable people. Do your research before paying for advice and ask to speak with existing clients of the professional Coach.

One way you could determine good Coaching from bad would be to ask what value they can add to your business. Another way could be to ask when your business will see a financial return on the advice being given. The best way to find a reputable Coach is to ask someone you know and trust.

Secure funding: If you feel you have a great business idea but don't have the funds to get started, you can use the conventional approach and ask your bank (or equivalent lender). Work out how much money you will need to launch and sustain your business. Work out how long it will take you to start making a profit. Lenders are less interested in your new business success and more interested in you making your monthly repayments back to them. We used to say that when we are starting a business and looking for backers, we turn to the three F's - Family, Friends, and Fools!

That's meant as a joke, but it is true that you can start speaking with people you know before taking on expensive debt to get started.

Stay compliant: Understand the legal requirements for your chosen industry and make sure you comply. Take out insurance where needed. When you are compliant, you are meeting legal and regulatory requirements. It's your safety net, protecting you from falling foul of legal issues like licenses and paying the correct taxes properly and timely.

Learn and evolve: Continuous learning will be needed to make sure you stay ahead. Seek knowledge from other sources and keep evolving your business strategy if you find it necessary.

Add value: Put your customers at the heart of what you do. Add more in 'value' than you take in payment – The Go-Giver1 first law. Delivering excellent products or services and providing a first-class customer experience builds loyalty. It will also generate referrals and testimonials to help win more new business.

Sales and marketing: This is the number one thing that lets down new entrepreneurs. They have decided on their 'passion' and done everything in the previous steps that has been asked. Then, they sit back thinking "Build it and they will come" - reference to Field of Dreams (a great movie starring Kevin Costner). This needs a strong business development plan that specifically targets the people you wish to serve. How do we find them? We need to fish where our customers are swimming. Where do they spend time together? What do they read? To which groups do they belong? It needs a plan with multiple routes to market.

Conclusion: It takes perseverance and dedication but when you do it right it will change your destiny. Think less about how much money you can make and more about how you can serve people. I don't wake up each day and think, "How many people can I invoice today?" I think, "How many people can I help today?" And by sticking with this philosophy, I serve many people and send many invoices. Lead with 'value' first.

1The Go-Giver is a thought-provoking and inspiring book that offers valuable insights into business development and personal growth. Written by Bob Burg and John David Mann, this international bestseller presents a radically simple yet profound message: the key to success lies in giving, not taking.

Through the story of Joe, an ambitious young man seeking success, the book explores the concept of "giving first." It challenges the conventional wisdom that success is achieved through competition and self-promotion. Instead, it advocates for a mindset of service and generosity.

By focusing on giving value to others, the book argues, we ultimately create opportunities for ourselves. When we help others succeed, we build strong relationships, gain respect, and attract abundance into our own lives.

The Go-Giver is a must-read for anyone looking to improve their career, build stronger relationships, and achieve lasting success. It will also improve your chances of success when you start generating new income streams.

The Entrepreneurial Mindset

Entrepreneurship is a thrilling and rewarding journey, but it's not for the faint of heart. It requires a unique mindset, a willingness to take risks, and a relentless pursuit of opportunity. To succeed as an entrepreneur, you need to think differently than most people. You need to be able to see problems as opportunities, and to approach challenges with a sense of optimism and determination. You need to be willing to step outside of your comfort zone and embrace the unknown.

In this section, I'll share some tips on how to develop an entrepreneurial mindset. These tips are based on my own experiences as an entrepreneur, as well as the experiences of other successful entrepreneurs I've had the pleasure of working with.

Whether you're looking for a side hustle or a full-time venture, these tips will help you on your entrepreneurial journey.

The next section will cover starting an enterprise with a £500 budget – so we do not need to put the crown jewels at risk here.

Cultivate a growth mindset

A growth mindset is essential for entrepreneurs. It's the belief that your abilities can be developed through dedication and hard work. When you have a growth mindset, you're more likely to embrace challenges as opportunities for learning and growth. What we think about we bring about!

Embrace risk

You'll need to be comfortable with uncertainty and willing to take calculated risks. Remember, every successful entrepreneur has faced setbacks and failures along the way. We are referring here to risking a relatively small amount of money and later in the chapter, there are ideas on getting started with only £500.

Develop a strong work ethic

Success in entrepreneurship requires hard work and dedication. You'll need to be willing to put in the long hours, make sacrifices, and persevere through challenges.

Network and build relationships

Your network is your net worth. Building strong relationships with other entrepreneurs, mentors, and industry professionals can provide invaluable support, advice, and opportunities.

Never give up

The path to entrepreneurial success is often bumpy. There will be setbacks, challenges, and moments of doubt. But it's important to never give up on your dreams. Keep your eye on the prize and persevere through the tough times.

Seek mentorship

Find a mentor who can offer guidance, support, and advice. A mentor can help you navigate the challenges of entrepreneurship and avoid common pitfalls.

Believe in yourself

Self-belief is crucial for entrepreneurial success. Believe in your abilities and your vision for your business. When you believe in yourself, others will believe in you too. And, repeating a message stated many times earlier – if we believe we will be successful, there is far more likelihood that we will.

Embracing your passion

One of the most effective ways to cultivate an entrepreneurial mindset is to embrace your passion. What truly excites you? What do you love to do so much that you could spend hours doing it without getting bored? Once you identify your passion, the possibilities are endless.

Consider your hobbies and interests. Are you a foodie with a knack for creating delicious dishes? Perhaps you could start a catering business or a food blog. Do you have a passion for fitness? You might consider becoming a personal trainer or opening a fitness studio. Love writing? Freelancing or self-publishing could be your calling. Perhaps you play the guitar, if so, you could teach others how to master the instrument.

The key is to find a way to monetise your passion. Think about how you can offer value to others and turn your hobby into a sustainable business. Remember, it's not just about making money; it's about doing something you love and making a difference.

When you're passionate about what you do, it shows. Your enthusiasm and dedication will be infectious, attracting customers and clients. Plus, you'll be more motivated to overcome challenges and persevere through setbacks.

So, take some time to reflect on your passions. What truly lights you up? Once you identify your calling, start exploring ways to turn it into a business. The journey may not be easy, but it will be incredibly rewarding.

Understand the needs of the market

Once you know what your passion is, you need to understand the needs of the market. What problems are people facing? What solutions are they looking for? Once you understand what your prospective customer needs, you can start to develop products or services that meet those needs.

For example, let's take cooking, If you know that people are looking for healthy and convenient meal options, you could start a meal delivery service. Regarding fitness, if you know that people are looking for ways to get in shape without going to the gym, you could start an online fitness program. Regarding writing, if you know that people are looking for information on a particular topic, you could write an e-book or create a blog on that topic. Similarly, teaching a musical instrument could include online training videos – thereby expanding your reach beyond your local area.

Plan your entrepreneurial vision and build a strategy towards it

Once you understand the needs of the market and you have a product or service idea, and you have a business plan, you need to develop a strategy. Your strategy should take into account your business goals, your target market, your marketing strategy, and your financial projections.

Think about how much money you would like your enterprise to achieve in the first year. Then expand that to the second and third years. Think about what other services or products you could sell in addition to your main product or service – the up-sell. If that term is new to you, an example of an up-sell is the eponymous McDonalds question – "Would you like fries with that?" Reflect on what other products or services you could offer in addition to your main offering.

Consider the geographic area you would like to cover. Are there alliances you could make that would promote your business even further than you could do alone? How are you going to find customers? Perhaps you will have a website, have a LinkedIn profile for your business, attend networking events in your area (or online), advertise in a local magazine. Will your business mainly be to serve members of the public, or do you have something you could sell to local businesses?

It is important to have a clear vision for your business. What do you want to achieve? Once you have a clear vision, you can start making tactical steps regarding how to go about achieving it.

You also need to know how much you need to pay yourself. If it's a side-hustle it's for extra cash. But if you have stopped working or retired, you will still have domestic costs that need servicing. Lots of start-ups are cash-poor for at least six months so think about how you will manage financially.

You will have already calculated your on-going cost of living from the last chapter, Handling Finances. You will also know your current income level. It should be straightforward to work out what level of income from your side-hustle you would like to achieve.

Learn from your setbacks

Failure is an inevitable part of the entrepreneurial journey. It's not a sign of weakness or a reason to give up. When we were teaching our children to walk, we didn't stop when they fell. We didn't put the child on the shelf and write them off. We carried on and worked it through with them. That's the resilience we need as entrepreneurs. You will only be taking baby steps at first.

When you face a setback, take some time to reflect on what went wrong. Don't beat yourself up but try to identify the root causes of the problem. What could you have done differently? What lessons can you learn from this experience?

Failure is an opportunity to learn and grow. It's a chance to refine your strategy, improve your skills, and become a stronger entrepreneur.

Some of the most successful entrepreneurs have experienced multiple failures before achieving their breakthrough. Thomas Edison, for example, is famously known for his thousand failed attempts (or 999 ways NOT to do it) before inventing his first light bulb. His perseverance and ability to learn from his mistakes ultimately led to his success.

Please note that I said 'his' first light bulb because, of course, he did not invent the first light bulb – that was down to Joseph Swan.

Don't let setbacks define you. Instead, use them as stepping stones on your path to success. Embrace the challenges and learn from your experiences. With determination and resilience, you can overcome any obstacle and achieve your goals.

Here are some additional tips for developing an entrepreneurial mindset:

Be creative and innovative. Entrepreneurs are always looking for new and better ways to do things. Don't be afraid to think creatively and produce new ideas.

Be adaptable. The business world is constantly changing, so it's important to be adaptable and willing to change your plans as needed.

Be persistent. Entrepreneurship is a marathon, not a sprint. There will be times when you want to give up, but it's important to keep pushing forward.

Developing an entrepreneurial mindset takes time and effort, but it's worth it. With an entrepreneurial mindset, you can achieve anything you set your mind to.

The Entrepreneur Mindset – starting small

Getting started on a low budget

With a budget of £500, you have a few different options for how to make as much money as possible. Here are a few ideas:

Invest in yourself. This could mean taking a course to learn a new skill, buying books or resources to help you improve your existing skills, or attending a conference or networking event. By investing in yourself, you can make yourself more valuable in the job market or start your own business.

Here are some specific examples, with more detail, of how you can make money by starting a micro business with £500. There are plenty of opportunities to turn your ideas into a profitable venture.

Identify your skills and interests

We have mentioned previously that it would be a great idea to embrace your passion. A hobby perhaps, that you could turn into a money-earner? Baking cakes, playing piano, gardening, repairing vehicles, whatever it is you enjoy doing in your spare time.

Research low-cost business ideas

Once you've identified your skills and interests, research business ideas that align with them. Consider ideas that require minimal upfront investment and can be started from home. Here are a few examples:

Online freelancing

Freelancing offers a flexible and rewarding way to earn extra income from the comfort of your own home. If you have skills in writing, editing, graphic design, virtual assistance, or web development, you can offer your services on various freelancing platforms. To succeed as a freelancer, it's essential to build a strong portfolio that showcases your skills and expertise. Highlight your previous work, projects, and client testimonials. A well-curated portfolio can attract potential clients and demonstrate your capabilities.

Reliable internet connectivity is crucial for freelancing. Ensure you have a stable and high-speed internet connection to avoid disruptions and delays. Networking is also essential in the freelancing world. Connect with other freelancers, potential clients, and industry professionals through online communities and social media. Building relationships can lead to new opportunities and referrals.

Freelancing requires self-discipline and time management skills. Set clear goals, manage your workload effectively, and maintain a consistent work ethic. With dedication and perseverance, you can build a successful freelancing career and enjoy the flexibility and financial benefits it offers.

E-commerce store

Starting an e-commerce store can be a lucrative side hustle, especially in today's digital age. Platforms like Shopify and Etsy make it easier than ever to set up your own online shop and start selling products. One of the keys to success in e-commerce is finding a niche market. Instead of trying to compete with large retailers, focus on a specific product or target audience. This will help you stand out and attract customers who are passionate about your offerings.

Once you've identified your niche, curate a carefully selected product range. Whether you're selling handmade goods, digital products, or products you've sourced from suppliers, ensure that your offerings align with your brand and appeal to your target market. Building a strong online presence is essential for driving traffic to your store. Optimise your website for search engines, use social media to engage with your audience, and consider paid advertising to reach a wider audience.

Success in e-commerce takes time and effort. Be patient, experiment with different marketing strategies, and continuously improve your online store. With dedication and perseverance, you can turn your e-commerce venture into a thriving business.

Content creation

In today's digital age, content creation has become a popular and profitable extra income stream for those with a talent for writing. Whether you're passionate about cooking, technology, or personal finance, there's an audience out there waiting to hear your voice. By starting a blog, YouTube channel, or podcast, you can share your expertise, passions, or stories with the world. Build a loyal following by consistently producing high-quality content that resonates with your audience.

Once you've established a strong following, you can monetise your content through various methods. Advertising, sponsorships, and affiliate marketing are common ways to generate income from your content. A successful content creation business takes time and effort to build. Be patient, consistent, and always strive to improve your craft.

Social Media management

Social media has become an essential tool for businesses and individuals alike. If you have a knack for creating engaging content and building online communities, offering social media management services can be a lucrative extra income. As a social media manager, you can help clients develop and implement effective social media strategies. This includes creating high-quality content, managing social media accounts, engaging with followers, and analysing performance metrics.

By providing valuable services, you can help businesses increase brand awareness, generate leads, and drive sales. As you build a reputation for your expertise, you can attract more clients and increase your earning potential.

To get started, create a portfolio showcasing your social media management skills. Network with businesses and individuals in your industry to build relationships and generate leads. Continuously stay updated on the latest social media trends and best practices to provide exceptional services to your clients. With dedication and hard work, you can turn social media management into a thriving business that generates significant income.

Virtual tutoring

If you have a passion for teaching and a knack for explaining complex subjects, virtual tutoring can be a rewarding and flexible way of earning extra income. With online platforms like Zoom and Skype, you can connect with students from around the world and share your knowledge. To get started, create a profile on a tutoring platform or establish your own online presence. Highlight your qualifications, experience, and the subjects you're able to teach. You can also create sample lessons or videos to showcase your teaching style.

Once you've built a reputation as a reliable and effective tutor, you can start charging for your services. Set your rates based on your experience, the subject matter, and the level of tutoring you offer. In addition to live tutoring sessions, you can also create and sell online training videos. Record yourself teaching a particular subject and offer the videos for download on your website or through platforms like Udemy or Teachable. This allows you to reach a wider audience and generate passive income.

Virtual tutoring offers a flexible way to earn extra income while helping students achieve their goals. With the right approach and dedication, you can build a successful tutoring business and make a positive impact on the lives of your students.

Handmade goods

Selling handmade goods can be a fulfilling and profitable side hustle. Whether you're a skilled crafter or simply enjoy creating unique items, there's a market for your products. From jewellery and pottery to baked goods and artwork, there's a wide range of handmade items that people are eager to purchase. Consider your skills and interests to determine what you'd like to create.

Once you've decided on your products, it's time to find your customers. Local markets and craft fairs are great places to showcase your work and connect with potential buyers. Online marketplaces like Etsy and eBay can also help you reach a wider audience. Building a successful handmade business takes time and effort. Focus on creating high-quality products, building a strong brand, and providing excellent customer service. With dedication and passion, you can turn your handmade creations into a thriving business.

Photography or videography services

If you have a passion for photography or videography, you can turn your hobby into a profitable income stream. Offer your services for events like weddings, birthdays, or corporate functions. You can also specialise in portrait photography or product photography.

To build your client base, network with local businesses, event planners, and individuals. Create a professional portfolio showcasing your best work and share it on social media. Consider offering special packages or discounts to attract new clients. Continuously improve your skills, invest in quality equipment, and provide excellent customer service to build a positive reputation.

Consulting services

If you have a deep understanding of a particular subject, consider offering your expertise as a consultant. This could involve providing guidance, advice, or solutions to individuals or businesses in your area of specialisation. To get started, identify your niche and target potential clients. Network with industry professionals, build a strong online presence, and create a portfolio showcasing your work.

When working with clients, be sure to listen carefully to their needs and tailor your advice accordingly. Demonstrate your expertise and provide valuable insights that can help them achieve their goals. As you build your reputation as a trusted consultant, you can increase your rates and attract more high-paying clients. Consulting can be a flexible and rewarding way to earn additional income while leveraging your skills and knowledge.

App development

In today's mobile-centric world, app development offers a lucrative opportunity for those with coding skills. Even if you're just starting out, you can leverage no-code or low-code platforms to create and launch your own app. These platforms provide a user-friendly interface that allows you to build apps without extensive coding knowledge. While they may have limitations compared to traditional coding, they offer a great starting point for aspiring app developers.

Once you've created your app, you can monetise it through various channels, such as in-app purchases, advertisements, or subscriptions. The key is to identify a target audience and develop an app that meets their needs and solves a problem. Success in app development requires creativity, technical skills, and a willingness to learn and adapt. Stay up to date with industry trends and user feedback to continuously improve your app and attract more users.

Freelance writer

Unleash your inner wordsmith and explore the world of freelance writing as an income stream. If you have a knack for crafting compelling content, this could be the perfect way to turn your passion into profit.

Several platforms connect freelancers with clients, like Upwork, Freelancer.com, and Fiverr. These platforms allow you to browse writing jobs, submit proposals, and build your portfolio. However, don't limit yourself to these marketplaces. Reach out directly to businesses and individuals in your area of expertise. Many websites and publications are constantly seeking fresh content, from blog posts and product descriptions to website copy and social media captions.

The key to success in freelance writing lies in showcasing your skills and establishing yourself as a reliable writer. Demonstrate your versatility by creating high-quality samples that cater to different needs. Building strong relationships with clients and exceeding expectations will not only get you repeat business but also lead to positive referrals.

Writing and selling e-books

If you have a passion for writing and sharing your knowledge, consider writing and selling e-books. With the rise of digital publishing platforms, it's easier than ever to create and distribute your own e-books. Choose a topic that you're knowledgeable about and passionate about. This will make the writing process more enjoyable and help you create a high-quality product.

Once you've chosen your topic, start outlining your e-book. Break it down into chapters or sections to organise your content. Then, begin writing, focusing on providing value and engaging your readers. Once your e-book is complete, you can self-publish it on platforms like Amazon Kindle Direct Publishing, Apple Books, or Smashwords. These platforms handle distribution, marketing, and payments, so you can focus on writing more content.

Drop shipping business

Drop shipping offers a great way to start an online business with minimal upfront investment. Unlike traditional e-commerce models, you don't need to stock or ship products yourself. When a customer places an order, you simply forward the order to your supplier, who will ship the product directly to the customer.

This model allows you to focus on marketing and customer service while minimising your financial risk. However, it's important to choose reliable suppliers and carefully manage your inventory and pricing. To start a drop shipping business, you'll need to create an online store (using platforms like Shopify or WooCommerce), research and select products to sell, partner with suppliers, and implement a marketing strategy to attract customers.

Affiliate marketing

To get started with affiliate marketing, you'll need to find products or services that align with your audience and niche. Once you've selected your affiliate partners, you can promote their products or services through your content. This could involve writing product reviews, creating tutorials, or sharing your personal experiences.

When someone clicks on your affiliate link and makes a purchase, you'll earn a commission. The commission rate varies depending on the product or service and the affiliate program.

Affiliate marketing can be a great way to earn passive income, but it requires consistent effort and a strong online presence. By building a loyal audience and creating high-quality content, you can increase your chances of success.

Public speaking

If you have a knack for captivating audiences and delivering engaging presentations, consider offering your services to conferences, events, and businesses. Think about your area of expertise from your current job (or the job you retired from) and target relevant conferences and events.

When preparing your presentation, focus on delivering value to your audience. Share your knowledge, insights, and experiences in a clear and engaging manner. Practice your delivery to ensure confidence and fluency. Once you've established yourself as a sought-after speaker, you can start charging for your services. The fees you can command will depend on your experience, topic, and the size of the audience.

Flip items

Flipping items can be a fun and rewarding way to earn extra income. It involves buying items at a low price and then selling them for a profit. You can find potential items to flip at thrift stores, garage sales, online marketplaces, or even in your own home. When selecting items to flip, focus on items that are in high demand and in good condition. Research current market prices to ensure you're buying at a fair price and setting a competitive selling price.

Once you've acquired your items, take high-quality photos and write detailed descriptions to attract potential buyers. Consider using platforms like eBay, Facebook Marketplace, or Etsy to sell your items. Just remember to do your research, negotiate good deals, and provide excellent customer service.

Rent out your spare room

If you have an extra room in your home, consider renting it out to generate some extra income. Platforms like Airbnb make it easy to list your space and connect with potential guests. Renting out a room can be a convenient and flexible way to earn additional income. You can set your own rates, choose your preferred guests, and maintain control over your living space.

Remember to consider local regulations and tax implications before renting out your room. It's also important to screen potential guests to ensure a positive experience for both you and your tenant. By renting out your spare room, you can turn an unused space into a source of income while meeting new people and potentially making lasting connections.

Rent out your car

If you have a car that sits idle most of the time, renting it out can be a great way to generate passive income. Platforms like Turo make it easy to list your car for rent and connect with potential renters. To get started, you'll need to provide information about your car, including its make, model, year, and mileage. You'll also need to set your rental rates and availability. Once your car is listed, renters can book it through the platform.

As a car owner, you'll typically receive a portion of the rental fee, minus platform fees and insurance costs. However, it's important to ensure your car is in good condition and that you have adequate insurance coverage.

Rent out your car parking space

If you live in a major city where parking is scarce and expensive—like London—you could make extra income by renting out your unused parking space.

Many commuters, residents, and businesses are willing to pay for a secure and convenient spot, especially in high-demand areas near transport hubs, offices, or shopping districts.

Platforms like **JustPark, YourParkingSpace**, and **Parklet** make it easy to list your space, set your price, and manage bookings. Prices vary based on location, but in prime areas, you could earn hundreds of pounds per month. It's a hassle-free way to generate passive income while helping others find affordable parking.

Exercise to help you decide which business to start:

Take a pen and paper and sit somewhere quiet. Then start writing what comes to mind with the following prompts.

Part 1: Your skills and experience

Experience: List your professional and life experiences. Consider all roles, volunteer work, hobbies, and significant life events. What skills did you develop?

Skills: From your experience inventory, identify your transferable skills. These are skills applicable across different industries and roles. Examples: communication, problem-solving, project management, teaching, sales, technical expertise, creative abilities, networking.

Network: Think about the people you know – former colleagues, friends, family, community members. Who are your connections in different industries or who might be potential customers or mentors? Write down key names or groups of people.

Part 2: Market opportunities & your interest

Market: Brainstorm current trends, emerging needs, or problems that you observe in the market. Consider both consumer needs (e.g., sustainable products, personalised services, convenience) and business needs (e.g., consulting, specialized training).

Interest: What are you passionate about? What do you enjoy doing? Starting a business requires dedication, so aligning it with your interests is crucial for long-term success.

Matching: Connect your skills and experience (Part 1) with the market opportunities and your interests (Part 2). Where do these areas overlap? These intersections are potential goldmines for business ideas.

Part 3: Business idea

Based on the matches you identified, generate specific business ideas. Don't censor yourself at this stage; write down everything that comes to mind. If you need help with this, there is guidance in this chapter, before this exercise and later.

Refinement & Research: Refine your top idea based on the evaluation. Conduct market research to validate your assumptions and identify your target audience.

Leveraging Your Age: Highlight your experience and maturity as assets. Many clients and customers value the wisdom and reliability that come with age.

Technology & Learning: Embrace technology but don't feel pressured to master everything at once. Focus on the tools that are essential for your business.

Additional Tips

Create a strong brand: Develop a memorable brand identity and a professional online presence.

Network with others: Connect with like-minded individuals and potential clients through online communities and networking events.

Continuously learn and improve: Stay updated on industry trends and invest in your professional development.

Be patient: Building a successful income stream takes time. Don't get discouraged by setbacks and keep pushing forward.

With the right mindset and a willingness to put in the effort, you can turn your side project into a thriving business. Don't forget the mindset!

In fact, it is worth repeating a main theme in this book – it's really all about mindset. If you think doing all this is too difficult and it is doomed to fail – then it will. However, **when you believe in yourself** and your ideas, your new micro business will take off and reward you with everything you want.

Minimise costs

To maximise your profit with a limited budget, keep your costs as low as possible. Consider using free or low-cost tools and resources for things like website creation, marketing, and design.

Leverage your network

Let your friends, family, and colleagues know about your new venture. Word-of-mouth marketing can be a powerful tool for generating initial customers. And when they have experienced your product or service, they can become ambassadors for your business and spread the word.

Utilise social media

Social media is a free and effective way to reach potential customers and promote your business. Create profiles on relevant platforms and share your content regularly. When you are generating profit, you can re-invest some of it back into this by paying someone to do this for you. You could use Fiverr or some other freelance platform like that.

Offer value

Focus on providing value to your customers. This could mean offering high-quality products or services, excellent customer service, or helpful information and resources. In fact, we have already mentioned The Go-Giver earlier in this chapter. I would go as far as to say, that if you don't know how you add value to the life of your customer, please do not bother them with your interruption. We are only in business to add value to people.

Reinvest your profits

As your business starts to generate income, reinvest some of your profits back into it. This could mean upgrading your equipment, hiring help, or expanding your offerings.

Case study: The gardener

One of the most pleasant clients I've worked with in my consultancy business was a young man who came to me when he was around 18 years old. He had no money so I gave him business growth advice for free. His enthusiasm for his work was infectious and I just had to help him.

He told me that before his sixteenth birthday, his father asked him what he wanted as a present. The young man said, "a lawn mower". Although his father was sceptical, sure enough, on the day of his birthday, the young man received a lawn mower.

When he had practiced with it, he wheeled it around the housing estate he lived on, knocking on doors and asking if they needed their garden tidying (yard work for my American friends). He carried on until he could afford to buy a van and then he spread his route further afield, picking up more and more regular clients as he went. That was because he was passionate about his work and loved every minute of his job.

After a couple of years, he started employing staff, investing in more machinery, more vehicles and found even more clients.

That was when he contacted me the first time and his free consultancy sessions were held in my kitchen. I provided guidance in the shape of a growth plan, showing him how we could expand his business profitably and provided the strategy and tactical plan that would see him reach a £250,000 sales income with around three staff and generate around 20% net profit. The young man took away the plans and got to work on them.

Around seven years later, he made contact again. This time he was in trouble because the business was leaking money and he was struggling to pay the staff each month. He still couldn't afford consultancy services so I tapped into some local business growth funding for him and we used that to provide me a small monetary reward for my time.

By now, his skills and the skills of his team were much higher. I advised he only bid for larger project work like landscaping gardens and that his lower end should be projects starting at £30,000. And we made every project carry its own Profit & Loss account. That way, we could see where he was losing money. Operational procedures were formalised so that the staff could follow easy instructions. Vans could not set off from the depot in the morning unless they had everything loaded that they would need for the day, stopping the need for backward and forward travel whilst working on a live project. We also invested in e-commerce so that clients could buy gardening products from his website – earning him money whilst he slept.

By 2023, coming up to age 30, the young man had a business plan that would take him to £1M turnover with his ten staff.

The moral of the story? This young man had a tremendous amount of faith in himself. He knew he didn't fit in at school and he didn't try to fight it. He simply left school when he could and started working for himself. He was not afraid to ask for help when he needed it. And he listened to that advice and acted on it. His passion remains intact and it remains infectious.

I wanted to share that with you because it shows how far you can take a side hustle. He went from earning pocket money to being a local employer.

Now, you may not wish to toil in gardens! That's OK. Just realise what can be achieved when you start with a small investment and spend years on a project for which you have a passion.

I also realise that my client was at the opposite end of his working life, compared with all of us nearing pensionable age or already drawing pensions. But I feel it needs including because you can choose something you are passionate about and literally make a business from the ground up, starting with nothing.

Conclusion

Which option is best for you will depend on your skills, interests, and risk tolerance. If you're not sure where to start, I recommend doing some research and talking to other entrepreneurs. Completing the exercise earlier in this chapter will also provide guidance.

Starting a side hustle with limited funds is challenging but achievable. By identifying your skills and interests, creating a solid business plan, and utilising free or low-cost resources, you can turn your ideas into a profitable venture. With hard work, dedication, and a willingness to learn, you can build a successful income stream and achieve your financial goals.

AI: A silver lining for entrepreneurial pensioners

With the rise of artificial intelligence (AI), pensioners are finding new and exciting ways to start their own businesses.

AI can be a powerful tool for the elderly looking to launch a venture. It can automate tasks, analyse data, and even provide customer service. For example, a retired accountant could use AI to develop a financial planning app, while a former teacher might create an online tutoring platform.

One of the biggest advantages of AI is that it can help to bridge the digital divide. AI-powered tools can make it easier to learn new technologies and stay up to date with the latest trends. Additionally, AI can help to reduce the workload, allowing you to focus on the creative and strategic aspects of your business.

Depending on what type of business you are creating, you may be able to use AI as a tool to help you create the content for your business. Below are some ideas for you in this regard.

The beauty of AI is that it will assist you in your learning of AI. If you are unsure of what to ask it, simply tell it you are unsure of how to write the prompt and tell it what you are trying to achieve. The more direction you can provide (by way of your needed outcomes), the better your results will be.

Before we see the list of 20 ideas, let me declare that I used AI to create the list! As I'm writing, AI is relatively new. Rather than explain how I used AI to form this list I will try to give a broader explanation – because things could be completely different in AI in as little as two years from now.

The user needs to provide a prompt, asking the system for a specific output. In the IT world many decades ago, we used to say, "crap input, crap output". Meaning, if we programme the machine badly, we will have poor results. This is exactly the same in AI. But the difference is, these days we can ask AI to help us with our initial prompt. We can 'talk' to the machine as if it were human and ask it what we should do.

For example, let's say we wanted to have an automated process to be able to ask people if they would like to benefit from our Reiki healing practice. We can type into AI, "Please tell me how I should ask for help with finding clients within 50 miles from my house, for my Reiki healing business. I want the process to be automated." You will receive a suggested prompt and you then use that prompt. You can continue to adjust your prompt dependent on the output you are looking for and only stop the re-iteration when you are happy with the result. In the list below, they are only ideas. You could take one or more of them and use them as AI prompts to build a whole business strategy, marketing plan, prospect list and sales plan. Then set to work.

So, here we go with some ideas on AI - generated by AI. What a strange world!

20 Creative businesses using artificial intelligence:

AI-powered content creation

Generate blog post outlines, product descriptions, or social media captions with AI writing tools.

Use AI art generators to create visuals for your content (illustrations, product mock-ups).

AI-enhanced social media management

Schedule posts and analyse social media data with AI tools for businesses.

Use AI chatbots to answer customer inquiries on social media platforms.

AI-driven data analysis

Offer freelance data analysis services using AI tools to extract insights for businesses.

Help small businesses personalise marketing campaigns using AI-powered customer segmentation.

AI-supported virtual assistant services

Use AI-powered scheduling tools and language models to provide virtual assistant services.

Offer transcription services with the aid of AI transcription software.

AI-powered tutoring and education

Develop online courses using AI-generated quizzes and personalised learning pathways.

Use AI chatbots to provide personalised tutoring or language learning support.

AI-generated product design and prototyping

Design and prototype simple products using AI 3D modelling tools.

Use AI to optimise product packaging and visual appeal for e-commerce businesses.

AI-assisted stock market analysis

Develop a niche blog or social media channel using AI-powered stock market analysis tools.

Offer AI-generated stock market insights as a paid subscription service (disclaimer: consult financial regulations).

AI-powered translation services

Offer translation services with the support of AI translation tools (ensure fluency in both languages).

Create multilingual content for businesses using AI translation engines and proofreading.

AI-enhanced customer support

Develop chatbots for customer support using AI conversation tools.

Offer training services for businesses on implementing AI-powered customer support solutions.

AI-generated music composition

Use AI music composition tools to create royalty-free music for content creators.

Offer AI-generated sound effects and background music for video projects.

AI-powered personalised fitness coaching

Develop a fitness app that uses AI to generate personalised workout plans.

Offer AI-powered virtual fitness coaching sessions using fitness trackers and analysis tools.

AI-assisted creative writing

Use AI story generators to spark creative ideas or overcome writer's block.

Edit and polish creative writing projects with the help of AI grammar and style checkers.

AI-powered market research

Conduct market research using AI sentiment analysis tools and social media data interpretation.

Offer AI-generated market research reports to businesses.

AI-supported search engine optimisation (SEO)

Use AI tools to analyse keywords and optimise website content for search engines.

Offer freelance SEO services with the help of AI-powered keyword research and competitor analysis tools.

AI-generated e-commerce product descriptions

Use AI tools to create compelling and informative product descriptions for online stores.

Optimise product descriptions for search engines with the help of AI keyword suggestion tools.

AI-powered video editing

Use AI-powered video editing tools to create engaging video content for social media or marketing purposes.

Offer AI-assisted video editing services to businesses or content creators.

AI-driven lead generation

Develop targeted advertising campaigns using AI audience segmentation tools for businesses.

Offer lead generation services for businesses using AI-powered marketing platforms.

AI-supported programming and coding

Use AI code completion and auto-suggestion tools for faster and more efficient programming.

Offer freelance coding services with the help of AI development tools (ensure your own coding skills are strong).

AI-powered personal finance management

Develop a budgeting app using AI to analyse spending habits and suggest financial goals.

Offer AI-powered financial planning consultations based on data analysis. (Disclaimer: consult financial regulations).

AI-generated personalised learning games

Develop educational games that use AI to adapt to the player's learning level and style.

Offer custom educational game development services for schools or educational institutions.

For some of these business ideas, you might need additional skills or background knowledge. However, AI can be a powerful tool to enhance your existing skills and explore new ways to make money.

Summary

This is such a 'mind-blowing' concept for some people, I feel the summary to this chapter needs to be more of a recap of some of the ideas. Just in case it is taking time for them to sink in.

There are many ways to create additional income streams, even on a limited budget. Some ideas might prompt you to get started – or even give you the inspiration to follow one of your own ideas.

Regardless of your age, you could earn money if that's what you would really like. I know it will not be straightforward but I also know that you could do it if the will was there.

Some of the suggestions above were for passive income streams – earning money while you sleep. You could set up any number of these and reach your desired income.

Creating additional income streams

Consider what skills and knowledge you've acquired throughout your life. Could you offer your expertise as a consultant, tutor, or mentor? Perhaps you have a talent for writing, editing, or graphic design that you could turn into a freelance business.

Many businesses can be run from the comfort of your own home. Consider starting a small business selling handmade goods, offering virtual services, or providing a unique product or service.

If you have extra space in your home, consider renting it out. This could include a spare room, basement, or garage. Platforms like Airbnb can help you connect with potential renters.

Utilise online platforms to offer your services as a freelancer. There are opportunities in various fields, including writing, editing, graphic design, virtual assistance, and many more.

Creating additional income streams takes time and effort. Be patient, persistent, and willing to adapt your approach as needed.

Unleash your inner businessperson

We have spoken of switching your way of thinking to that of an entrepreneur. To succeed in creating additional income streams, it's essential to adopt an entrepreneurial mindset. Here are some key characteristics to cultivate:

Entrepreneurs are willing to take calculated risks to pursue their goals. Be open to trying new things and don't be afraid to step outside your comfort zone.

Entrepreneurs are skilled at identifying problems and finding innovative solutions. Cultivate your problem-solving abilities to overcome challenges and seize opportunities.

The business landscape is constantly changing. Be adaptable and willing to adjust your plans as needed.

Entrepreneurship can be a rollercoaster ride. Develop resilience and the ability to bounce back from setbacks.

Build strong relationships with other entrepreneurs, mentors, and potential clients. Networking can provide valuable opportunities and support. You will find plenty of like-minded business owners online – a great place to network and share ideas.

A genuine passion for your business will fuel your motivation and drive. Let your enthusiasm shine through in your work.

Put your customers first and strive to provide exceptional value. Understanding your customers' needs and preferences is essential for success.

By embracing these entrepreneurial traits, you'll be well-equipped to create and grow a successful side hustle.

Tips for the frugal start-up

Starting a business doesn't require a lot of capital. With a limited budget, you can still launch a successful venture. Here are some of the ideas shared earlier.

Be mindful of your expenses and find ways to cut costs. Consider working from home, using free or low-cost tools, and networking with other entrepreneurs to share resources.

Begin with a small-scale operation and gradually expand as your business grows. This allows you to manage your resources effectively and minimise risk.

Take advantage of online platforms to reach a wider audience and reduce overhead costs. Consider selling your products or services online, using social media to promote your business, and building a website.

Connect with experienced entrepreneurs who can offer guidance and support. Mentorship can provide valuable insights and help you avoid common pitfalls.

Believe in yourself. As we have seen in everyday life, confidence and a positive mindset are essential for creating a positive life and entrepreneurial success. Believe in your abilities and your potential to succeed.

The key to starting a successful business on a low budget is creativity, resourcefulness, and a willingness to learn and adapt. With the right mindset and strategies, you can turn your ideas into a thriving venture.

Resource for starting and growing a business

If you would like help regarding starting a business or expanding the business you already have, then please take a look at my Lightworker Coach website – www.lightworkercoach.co.uk where you will find resources to help you. There are online training courses you can download that will help you get started in your business and show you ways to find your customers. You will notice the focus is on starting specific types of businesses, those that are 'heart-led'. But the principles are the same for any business. Besides, it might convince you to start a business that resonates with your soul – and I would love to see more of those!

Then, once you have surplus cash you may wish to become a philanthropist and start giving back to society. There are lots of ways you can do this and not all of them require you giving away money.

In the next chapter we will explore together some ways in which you might wish to give back to society.

Chapter 7 – Giving Back

"The best way to find yourself is to lose yourself in the service of others."

Mahatma Gandhi

Making a lasting impact

As we reach the age of 60, we've often accumulated a wealth of knowledge, experience, and wisdom. It's a time to reflect on our journey and consider how we can make a lasting impact on the world. Giving back is a powerful way to contribute to society, find purpose, and enrich our own lives.

Giving back can provide a sense of purpose and fulfilment, especially during retirement. It can help us feel connected to our community and make a positive difference in the lives of others. Giving back can be a great way to meet new people and build lasting relationships and social connections. It's an opportunity to connect with like-minded individuals who share your values and passions.

Studies have shown that volunteering can have a positive impact on our mental and physical health, thereby improving our well-being. It can reduce stress, boost our mood, and even increase our lifespan. Giving back can help us create a lasting legacy. By contributing to causes we care about, we can leave a positive impact on future generations.

There are countless ways to give back to your community. You can freely give your time at a local charity, non-profit organisation, or community centre. Perhaps you would like to mentor people, sharing your knowledge and experience by helping young people or aspiring professionals.

If you are abundant in terms of money but short on time it could be that donating is your chosen route. Donate to causes you care about, whether it's financially or through in-kind donations. Consider establishing a charitable foundation or endowment to support causes you believe in.

Leaving a legacy is about more than just material possessions. It's about the impact we make on the world and the people around us. By giving back, we can create a lasting legacy that will be remembered long after we're gone.

The key to meaningful giving is to find something that you're passionate about. What causes do you care deeply about? What skills and experiences can you offer? Once you've identified your passion, you can start exploring opportunities to give back.

No matter how big or small your contribution, every act of giving has the potential to make a difference. It's not about the amount you give, but the love and compassion behind it.

By giving back, we not only enrich the lives of others but also enrich our own. It's a powerful way to find meaning, purpose, and fulfilment in our later years.

Subjects in this chapter:

- Leaving a Legacy
- Volunteer work
- Discover your passion

Creating a legacy

Have you ever wondered about the mark you'll leave on the world? Your legacy isn't just about the things you accumulate, but the impact you make on humanity. It's about the stories you create, the values you uphold, and the change you set in motion.

What is a legacy? Well, one way to answer that might be to say that it's a story that extends beyond your lifetime.

A legacy is more than a material inheritance. It's the lasting impression you leave, the stories that continue to inspire, and the positive change you've brought about.

At its core, creating a legacy means making a long-term difference. It's about being remembered for your contributions, values, and the positive change you brought into the lives of others.

Your legacy is not just about grand gestures or immense wealth. It's in the little acts of kindness, the knowledge you share, the values you uphold, and the relationships you nurture. It's the way you treat people, the lessons you teach, and the inspiration you ignite. Whether you are a parent passing on values to your children or an entrepreneur transforming a community, you are crafting your legacy.

Before we get started on what it is to have a legacy and how we might go about starting one, I just want to ask some questions of you:

What would you like people to remember you by?

What is your purpose? You may not know right now.

What, in your opinion, is wrong that you might wish to put right?

These are all important questions to ask ourselves, especially as we get older. We all want to leave a mark on the world, to make a difference in some way. But how do we do that? Well, one way would be to use what you love to put right what you dislike – what could you do to combat whatever it is that you want to correct?

What do you feel sickened by when you see it on TV or in the newspaper? It might be child poverty, cruelty to animals, correcting the education system, ending wars, ending corruption in politics, eradicating racism, empowering women and so on.

Please take a moment right now and write down your thoughts in this regard. Focus on one issue that you wish to address and then list the ways in which you think you could make a positive difference to that issue.

Finding your passion

To create a meaningful legacy, you might start going about it another way, like starting by identifying your passions. What truly excites you? What causes do you care about? When you align your actions with your values, your legacy becomes an authentic reflection of who you are.

Making a difference

Consider how you can contribute to your community, industry, or society at large. Your impact could be as simple as mentoring a young person or volunteering for a cause you believe in.

Storytelling and wisdom

Your life experiences are a treasure trove of wisdom. Sharing your stories can inspire and guide others. Whether through writing, speaking, or informal conversations, pass on your lessons, insights, and experiences.

Creating a lasting impact

Legacy isn't bound by time. It's about the positive changes you inspire, and the lives you touch. Focus on making a difference, no matter how small. Your legacy is a testament to the choices you've made and the impact you've had on the world.

Sustainable living

In today's world, sustainability is increasingly important. Consider how your choices impact the environment and future generations. Embracing sustainable practices can be a powerful way to create a positive legacy.

Giving back

Philanthropy can be a meaningful way to give back to your community and support causes you care about. Consider donating your time, money, or resources to organisations that align with your values.

Living authentically

Your legacy is shaped by your daily choices and actions. Strive to live authentically, embracing your true self. When you live with integrity and purpose, your legacy becomes a reflection of your character.

Inspiring others

Your legacy can inspire others to follow in your footsteps. Share your story, celebrate your achievements, and encourage others to pursue their own passions. By inspiring others, you create a wave of positive change.

Why is creating a legacy important?

Creating a legacy is important because it gives your life meaning. It shows that you have made a difference in the world. It also gives you something to strive for, something to work towards.

Part of creating a legacy is sharing your story. Your experiences, successes, failures, and lessons learned are a treasure trove of wisdom. Passing on this knowledge helps future generations navigate their own paths. Whether through writing, speaking, or even informal conversations, your stories become a beacon of guidance.

Sure, you might leave some people an amount of money. But setting up an institute to do magnificent work and having people work on your ideas, such that your institute lasts 50, 100 or even 200 years – that is a legacy.

Exercise: Crafting your legacy

This exercise is designed to help you reflect on your life and values, and to articulate the kind of legacy you wish to leave behind.

Part 1: Reflecting on your life

Timeline of significance: Create a timeline of your life, highlighting key events, experiences, and relationships that have shaped you. Include both joyful moments and challenges you overcame.

Values exploration: List the core values that are most important to you. These might include things like honesty, kindness, creativity, resilience, family, community, knowledge, or spiritual faith. Reflect on how you have lived these values in the past.

Accomplishments & contributions: List your significant accomplishments and contributions, both personal and professional. These could be anything from raising a family to achieving a career goal to volunteering in your community. Don't minimize anything; acknowledge all the ways you've made a difference.

Part 2: Defining your legacy vision

Legacy brainstorm: Imagine yourself in the future, looking back on your life. What do you hope to have accomplished? What impact do you want to have made? What do you want people to remember about you? Write down as many ideas as you can, without censoring yourself.

Legacy themes: Review your brainstormed ideas and identify the key themes that emerge. These might relate to family, community, career, personal growth, social justice, or creative expression. These themes will form the foundation of your legacy vision.

Legacy Statement: Craft a short statement that summarises your desired legacy. This doesn't have to be formal or perfect; it's a personal guide for you. For example: "I want to be remembered as someone who lived with integrity, cherished her family, and made a positive impact on her community through her volunteer work and kindness."

Part 3: Action planning

Areas of focus: Based on your legacy statement, identify specific areas where you want to focus your energy and efforts in the coming years. These could be:

Strengthening bonds with family and friends. Sharing your wisdom and experience with younger generations. Volunteering your time or donating to causes you care about. Pursuing artistic or creative passions. Continuing to learn and grow.

Action Steps: For each area of focus, identify concrete action steps you can take to work towards your legacy vision. Be specific and realistic.

Legacy is often the reason we still celebrate historical figures, learn from ancient civilisations, and draw inspiration from our ancestors. Similarly, your legacy has the potential to transcend your years, becoming a source of inspiration for your children, grandchildren, and countless others who follow.

The four Ps of legacy

There are four key things to consider when creating a legacy:

Passion: What are you passionate about? What drives you? What do you love to do?

Purpose: What do you want to achieve with your life? What difference do you want to make in the world?

Path: How are you going to achieve your purpose? What steps are you going to take?

Plan: How are you going to make your legacy sustainable? How are you going to ensure that it continues to make a difference long after you are gone?

Things to consider in making a legacy

Creating a legacy will not be plain sailing. When you come to address large corporations or education authorities or government bodies or the justice system or any other faceless organisation, you will get push-back. They will explain how they are already resolving the issue of which you speak.

Make sure the intention of your legacy is pure. It will not get off the ground if there are any hidden agendas (like making money for you). Of course, funding needs to be found and that will happen. It's just that you need to be focused on helping others and not on financial gain.

Study other people who have left legacies by reading books and watching movies.

Building a lasting legacy: five key elements

Creating a legacy is about leaving a lasting impact on the world. It's not just about achieving something great but also ensuring that your legacy endures. To build a legacy that stands the test of time, there are five key elements to consider:

Longevity

How long will your legacy last? This depends on several factors, including the nature of your legacy, its sustainability, and the actions of future generations.

Choose a cause that matters: The more meaningful and impactful your cause, the more likely it is to endure.

Build a strong foundation: Ensure that your legacy is built on solid foundations, such as a well-established organisation or a sustainable business model.

Involve future generations: Encourage younger generations to carry on your legacy. Share your knowledge, inspire their passion, and involve them in your work.

Sustainability

A sustainable legacy is one that can be maintained over time. Consider the long-term implications of your actions and ensure that your legacy can be supported and continued by future generations.

Choose sustainable practices: If your legacy involves a business or organisation, ensure it operates sustainably. This could involve minimising environmental impact, promoting social responsibility, or using ethical business practices.

Diversify your income streams: If your legacy is based on financial contributions, diversify your income sources to ensure long-term sustainability.

Build a strong team: Surround yourself with a dedicated and passionate team who can carry on your legacy after you're gone.

Recruitment

How will you attract and retain the people who will help you build your legacy? Consider the skills, experience, and values you're looking for in your team.

Create a clear vision: Clearly articulate your vision for your legacy and how others can contribute to it.

Offer meaningful opportunities: Provide opportunities for growth, development, and recognition.

Foster a positive culture: Create a supportive and inclusive environment where people feel valued and appreciated.

Quality

The quality of your legacy is determined by its impact and value. Ensure that your work is of the highest standard and that it makes a positive difference in the world.

Set high standards: Strive for excellence in everything you do.

Seek feedback: Continuously seek feedback and make improvements based on the insights you receive.

Measure your impact: Track the outcomes of your work and assess its effectiveness.

Flexibility

The world is constantly changing, and your legacy must adapt to these changes. Be open to new ideas, embrace innovation, and be willing to adjust your plans as needed.

Stay informed: Keep up to date on industry trends and developments.

Be adaptable: Be willing to change your approach if necessary to achieve your goals.

Embrace innovation: Explore new technologies and strategies that can help you achieve your legacy.

By considering these five elements, you can build a lasting legacy that will continue to inspire and impact future generations. Remember, your legacy reflects your values, your passions, and your commitment to making a difference in the world.

Real Examples of People Who Created Legacies

There are many real examples of people who have created legacies that matter. Here are a few:

Mother Teresa

Mother Teresa, a Catholic nun of Albanian origin, devoted her life to serving the impoverished and suffering. She established the Missionaries of Charity, a religious order that provides care to those in need worldwide. Renowned for her unwavering compassion and selfless dedication, Mother Teresa established numerous shelters, orphanages, and soup kitchens across the globe. Her unwavering commitment to humanity earned her the Nobel Peace Prize in 1979, a testament to her extraordinary impact on the world. Mother Teresa's legacy continues to inspire millions, serving as a beacon of hope and compassion for generations to come.

Albert Einstein

Albert Einstein, a renowned physicist, revolutionized our understanding of the universe with his groundbreaking theory of relativity. His work, particularly his theories of special and general relativity, fundamentally changed our perception of space, time, gravity, and the cosmos. Einstein's insights have had far-reaching implications for fields such as astrophysics, cosmology, and navigation systems. His contributions to science are celebrated worldwide, and he is widely regarded as one of the greatest minds of the 20th century. In recognition of his extraordinary achievements, Einstein was awarded the Nobel Prize in Physics in 1921.

Martin Luther King, Jr.

Martin Luther King Jr. was a pivotal figure in the American Civil Rights Movement, championing equality and justice for all. His eloquent speeches, unwavering leadership, and peaceful protests inspired millions to fight for racial equality. King's most famous speech, "I Have a Dream," delivered at the March on Washington for Jobs and Freedom in 1963, articulated a vision of a society free from racial segregation and discrimination. This powerful address became a defining moment in the Civil Rights Movement, galvanizing support for the cause of racial equality.

Tragically, King was assassinated in 1968. However, his legacy continues to inspire and influence people around the world. His message of peace, love, and equality resonates with individuals of all backgrounds, reminding us of the importance of fighting for justice and human rights.

These are just a few examples and there are many thousands of others who are less well known. There are lots of people who have made a difference in the world, and their stories can inspire us to create our own legacies.

Making a positive contribution

Creating a legacy means focusing on the bigger picture – beyond immediate gratification. It is about asking yourself, "How can I contribute positively to the world?" This could involve sustainable practices, ethical business decisions, or philanthropy. By considering the long-term consequences of your actions, you shape a legacy that endures.

In the end, your legacy is not something you leave behind; it's something you build every day. It's a beautiful blend of personal growth, empathy, contribution, and connection. Whether through kindness, innovation, or compassion, your legacy becomes a gift to the world – a testament to the mark you made during your journey. So, embrace your uniqueness, live authentically, and let your legacy unfold as a tapestry of meaningful moments.

Creating the money your legacy will need

Corporate or event giving

One way to create the money your legacy will need is to secure corporate or event giving. This means approaching businesses or organisations and asking them to donate money to your cause. You can also organise fundraising events to raise money.

Set up an endowment

An endowment is a fund that is set up to provide financial support for a specific purpose. You can set up an endowment to support your legacy by donating money to a charity or university. The money in the endowment will be invested and the interest earned will be used to support your cause.

Will and trust funds

A will is a legal document that outlines how your assets will be distributed after your death. You can use a will to set up a trust fund for your legacy. A trust fund is a legal arrangement where a trustee manages assets on behalf of another person or organisation. The trustee will use the assets in the trust fund to support your cause.

Set up a non-profit organisation

Another way to create the money your legacy will need is to set up a non-profit organisation. A non-profit organisation is a legal entity that is exempt from paying taxes. Non-profit organisations can raise money through donations, grants, and other fundraising activities.

In the UK, this will most likely take the form of a CIC (Community Interest Company). CICs are limited companies which operate to provide a benefit to the community they serve. The purpose of a CIC is primarily one of community benefit rather than private profit.

People who have benefitted from the programme to give back

You can encourage graduates of the program to give back by donating money or volunteering their time. This can help to ensure that your legacy continues to make a difference even after you are gone.

The people that benefit from your programme (those that you have helped) will become walking advertisements of your legacy and will encourage people to make a donation.

Ambassador programme, where other people raise funds

You can also set up an ambassador program where other people raise funds for your legacy. This could involve setting up a website or social media campaign where people can donate money or volunteer their time.

Donations

Finally, you can simply ask people to donate money to your legacy. This could be done through a direct mail campaign, a website, or social media.

The best way to create the money your legacy will need will depend on your specific circumstances and goals. However, all of the methods mentioned above can be effective ways to raise money for your cause.

Creating a legacy that matters

When you want to measure the progress and success of your legacy, forget time and measure milestones. Count up the emotions of the people who have been moved by your legacy, rather than the money in the bank.

You will need to love people who might not deserve it. You will need to put yourself out there before anything might come back.

If the people on your team are not focused like you on bringing a benefit to humanity – then your legacy will fail.

Creating a legacy is a challenge, but it is also an incredibly rewarding experience. When you create a legacy, you are making a difference in the world. You are leaving your mark on history. So, what are you waiting for? Start creating your legacy today.

Raising Horizons

Why might I feel able to write about creating a legacy? Because I attended a retreat in The Bahamas that was a 'Legacy Retreat'. As a group, we planned for six days together so that each of us could launch our own legacy.

As a result of the retreat, I developed plans to create an institute called Raising Horizons, which will create a "5 Pillars to Raise Horizons" programme, where children who have zero financial support can help themselves and others to create a route to a financially successful life and raise the horizons of others like them.

The plan is to go into schools and find those children that would otherwise have no hope. They will be taught entrepreneurial skills to enable them to start their own business and they will be shown how to get themselves 'ready' for the workplace. We will engage with local businesses, who will take them in for work experience and, in the right circumstances, employ the person.

The children would be asked to commit to 'giving back' when they were well established. That would mean them being mentors to younger students and paying back financially for the support they received from the legacy. We would also tout for sponsorship from local businesses, educational establishments and local authorities. That way, we ensure the legacy endures beyond my passing.

I know what it is like to be hungry. We will take the kids after school and serve them food while they learn their new skills. The sessions will be called 'food for thought' and I am sure this one act will be enough to ensure we have high attendance at every session!

When I was ready, I got my plan together and started by contacting the mayor for my old home town and explained what I was going to attempt. He then said I should start with educationalists and he sent my plans to someone in his network. That is where the trail went cold. Then I realised that I needed to "sell" my plan to people who will say, "We already do that" and reject my plans before I'm given a chance to speak. So, I made a tactical retreat.

Then life as a primary carer got in the way and I needed to focus on being at home with my wife.

However, I set it out as an example of what a legacy might look like, the specific target group I wish to help, how it will fund itself and why I have a passion to help adolescent kids.

Why this legacy?

Why is this particular legacy a passion of mine?

You know my back story now about how I was raised as a child. Looking at where I most needed help it was from age 14. And the sort of help I needed was to be shown a path out of poverty. I was told as a child that I was useless and would amount to nothing, so I also needed someone who believed in me to raise my aspirations.

I have more recently realised that **the skills I have now would have been a benefit to my fourteen-year-old self**.

Now I would like to help those teenagers who are typically in single-parent homes or whose parents are unemployed or for other reasons, are living in poverty. In my home town there are often three generations of unemployed men – grandfather, father and son sitting watching daytime TV together. This provides the teenager with a very restricted view of the world and my expectation is that my legacy will allow these 'lost youths' to raise their horizons, taking them and their future offspring out of poverty. Their biggest lack is the lack of a role model. As you know, that was also the biggest single thing that hampered me when I was 14.

When you have nobody to look up to for guidance, inspiration and mentoring, as a boy going through puberty, it is very difficult to see how you are going to make a place in the world for yourself. Which creates tremendous anxiety and stress.

I would love to be that person who can lift the aspirations of that age range and show them there is something much better on the horizon. I can be the role model they might be seeking because I've been where they are right now and I raised myself above it.

They will be taught the lessons we have touched on in the last chapter, 'Start your own small business'.

I hope to have the time to invest in this legacy in the coming years.

Summary

Retirement offers a unique opportunity to give back to society and leave a lasting legacy. It's a time when many people have the freedom and flexibility to pursue their passions and make a difference in the world. Whether you're looking to volunteer your time, share your expertise, or simply make a donation, there are countless ways to contribute to your community.

Giving back

This isn't just about money or material possessions. It's about making a positive impact on the lives of others and creating a lasting memory. It's about leaving the world a better place than you found it.

One way to give back is through volunteering. By dedicating your time and energy to a cause you care about, you can make a real difference in the lives of those in need. Whether you're volunteering at a local food bank, mentoring young people, or working with animals, your contributions can have a profound impact.

Another way to give back is through mentorship. Sharing your knowledge and experience with younger generations can help them achieve their goals and make a positive impact on the world. By mentoring others, you're not only helping them succeed, but you're also passing on your values and wisdom.

You can give back through your charitable giving. By donating to causes you believe in, you can support important work and make a difference in the world. Whether you're making a one-time donation or establishing a charitable foundation, your generosity can have a lasting impact.

Finally, to can start your own legacy and set it up so that, after initial investment, it becomes self-funding. This can be achieved by asking the people who benefitted from your legacy programme to donate back to the legacy, once they have become established themselves.

Volunteer work

Volunteering is a great way to give back to your community and make a difference in the world. It's also a wonderful way to meet new people, learn new skills, and stay active.

There are countless volunteer opportunities available, so there's sure to be something that interests you. Whether you're passionate about environmental conservation, social justice, or animal welfare, there's a volunteer opportunity waiting for you.

Volunteering can also be a great way to stay mentally and physically active. It can help to reduce stress, improve your mood, and boost your self-esteem. Plus, it's a great way to meet new people and make friends.

If you're not sure where to start, there are many resources available to help you find volunteer opportunities. You can check with local charities, non-profit organisations, and government agencies. You can also search online for volunteer opportunities in your area.

Your reward

Of course, there does not need to be a reward for being charitable but you will feel much better about yourself when you are. It really is true when they say, "It is better to give than to receive."

Not only will you be remembered for a very long time where people will sing your praises but during your lifetime you will see the benefits that your giving back is creating and how it is changing people's lives for the better.

Helping other people helps to raise the vibration of the planet. When you feel you are able, please reach down and help someone else up. Even the smallest acts of kindness raise the collective mind of humanity and move us all on to higher levels of enlightenment.

So, we've seen the power of giving back to transform lives. But what fuels this desire to give? Where does this compassion originate? Could the answer lie in the realm of spirituality?

Let's delve deeper and see if we can find the answer together in the final chapter.

Chapter 8 – Embracing Spirituality

"What lies behind you and what lies in front of you, pales in comparison to what lies inside of you."

Ralph Waldo Emerson

As we reach our later years, many of us find ourselves drawn to explore spirituality more deeply. We begin to ponder bigger questions about the meaning of life, our purpose, and what lies beyond this physical existence. This spiritual curiosity is a beautiful part of the human journey, one that can bring profound wisdom, peace, and growth.

Here, we will embark on an insightful exploration of spirituality. We will delve into practices that can nurture your spiritual wellbeing, learn to find deeper fulfilment, and cultivate a greater connection with yourself and the world around you. Of course, spirituality is a highly personal experience, so approach this chapter with an open mind and take from it whatever resonates with you.

Subjects in this chapter:

- My own take on Spirituality
- Understanding Spirituality
- Practices for Spiritual Growth
- Living With Purpose and Presence
- Death, Dying and the Great Mystery

My own take on spirituality

Before we go deeper into this subject, I want to make sure it is understood that I have no personal 'axe to grind' about spirituality. If you are reading this and you believe in God, then nothing in this chapter (or indeed this book) is designed to shake your belief. In fact, I would like to think it might cement your relationship with your God.

However, religion did play a part in my early life. My father was raised a Methodist and so, naturally, that's the religion we followed. I attended church regularly and was part of the Cub Scouts and the Boy Scouts, which also meant church parades in our uniforms. By the time I was fifteen, I had volunteered to become a Sunday School teacher and I had a class that I looked after every Sunday morning.

Also, our church encouraged youngsters to read the Bible by offering a book token to any child who could pass scripture exams. We did not have any money for books at home so I spent lots of time after school in church reading scriptures to earn tokens that I could swap for books.

By the age of fifteen, I was starting to think for myself and noticed incongruities in my home and church life. It became apparent to me what the underlying tenet of the Methodist church was – sobriety. Yet my father was an alcoholic!

It's from those teenage years that religion unravelled for me. But because I read the Bible and attended scripture classes, I felt I knew a great deal about the messages in the writings and I understood what they were trying to achieve. Peace, love, kindness and compassion for our fellow humans.

Whereas I was experiencing nothing of this at home.

After leaving home

Since my teenage years I have travelled widely and now have Jewish friends, Muslim friends, and of course, Christian friends. So, I know that the prophets named and honoured in each of these three religions are the same! The Jewish scriptures (the Tanakh) and the Christian Old Testament and the Muslim Koran all revere the same prophets. Of the three religions, the Jewish faith was first, then their prophets are mentioned in the Christian bible and those prophets are mentioned in the Koran. Christians honour the Jewish prophets and then add their own, Christ, and Islam honours all the prophets in the Bible, and then add their own, Mohammed.

This is worth mentioning because it always makes me scratch my head at the futility and long history of fighting between these three religions. And more specifically, the similarity between Jewish people and Muslim people. They are more alike than they are disparate. It's exactly this that made me realise that I did not wish to align myself with any religious label. It feels like each kill the other in the name of their God and the messengers from that very God are the same on both sides of the battle!

Just for the record, I also have lots of Hindu friends but their narrative is different to that example above. And I learned when I visited India that they are the only country in the world that has an army but has never invaded any other country.

So, I spent my years between sixteen and my late sixties in what some might call 'the wilderness years'. Then, at sixty-eight, **something changed**.

My awakening

The world was in the middle of the Covid 19 pandemic. My consultancy practice which focuses on helping high growth businesses simply stopped. Nobody wanted people coming into their premises when we were in such nervous times and in lockdown. So, I accepted online work from an American guy who had international clients. The premise being that I would train in his methodology and then deliver that training to his clients in Europe and he would pay me for each online training class I delivered.

This new working relationship meant I spent a fair amount of time online speaking with the American trainer. In addition to providing his training, he spoke of leaving a legacy that will outlast us by many years – potentially hundreds of years. I was interested in this concept already so his message resonated with me. He held a retreat in The Bahamas that I attended and we all learned so much more about legacies and how we might start our own. He also told us that the trainers who took part in the legacy retreat would be those who he would look to give work to first. So, I went to that legacy retreat with the intention of getting more work and earning more money.

I want to underline that, if you don't mind. I went to the retreat with the intention that it would be rewarded financially.

There were around sixteen of us (when we include the delegates and the delivery team) and we would start each day in group meditation outside, at the edge of the ocean, on the lawn. The American trainer would lead the guided meditation. I had never meditated properly until that week in The Bahamas. I had tried. I had bought a book on the subject but it didn't help. I was simply unable to 'still' my mind from all the nonsense that my mind threw up. So, I simply put my trust in the process and followed instructions. Because we were in a guided meditation I think it was easier for me to go 'deep' just by listening to the voice and the backing track.

On the third of these group meditations, I had an experience that I find hard to explain. I found myself floating in a golden light and feeling completely relaxed and safe. The overriding emotion was love. I mean love for everyone and everything in the universe. I felt connected to everything on the planet at an atomic level. It seemed logical that I would be linked to everything because we are all made of the same things that make up everything on our planet and everything in the universe. It was a wonderful enlightening experience that seemed to go on for a long time. I felt overwhelmed with love and I was aware that I was loved, loving and lovable.

The whole group meditation lasted one hour and when it ended, I could not move or speak. Everyone else got up and went inside. One of the delegates seemed to notice my difficulty and she helped me walk back indoors. I just held her hand and leaned on her without either of us saying anything.

Everything in my life changed immediately after that enlightening meditation. The world seemed a much kinder, more loving place. I became more in tune with everyone else around me. I experienced more kindness – dare I say love – from the people attending the retreat. There were unexpected acts of kindness from strangers on flights and in the airports on my way home. I landed in Manchester, which meant I needed to drive across the Pennines to reach home. It was a beautiful sunny day and I can honestly say I have never seen the hills looking so stunning. It's hard to explain – everything was the same but different. I felt connected to it all.

Now I understand a lot more clearly my place in the world and I see how precious life is. And now I want to give back and help others raise their consciousness.

Now if I am asked, I say I am spiritual but not religious. I have no negativity toward anyone who is religious, most of whom are spiritual as well. I simply realise now that we don't need to visit a place of worship to engage with a Divine Spirit, we can find all we need inside of ourselves.

Although I had no idea what was happening to me at the time, when I started speaking about it to other spiritual people, they told me I had an awakening. I don't really know to this day what that means but I'm comfortable with being able to explain it in a few words – rather than being lost for words.

Two years after that retreat, I reached the age of 70. I consider that experience as being similar to a software upgrade. So, the recent trend in software is to call the latest version 2.0 or 3.0 – so now I consider myself as being Peter Allen Dickinson 7.0 – just for a bit of fun.

Lightworker Coach

Something else happened when I reached 70 – I started another business!

Because of my new-found spirituality, I seemed to be drawn to meet spiritual people. These are spiritual guides, healers, clairvoyants, psychics, seers and people who channel information from beyond the veil.

Collectively, these people are known as lightworkers.

Lightworkers have a deep desire to help others. They are committed to serving the needs of humanity. They are people who are guided by their inner feelings and instincts. They have a special ability, call it intuition, to understand how others are feeling and what they need. This helps them use their healing energy to help people who are struggling. Lightworkers also believe in working together to spread positive energy and healing, which can help to overcome negativity in the world.

A great many of these people have given up their day job to pursue their aspirations to help people. They start their own small business and charge a small amount of money, simply as an 'energy exchange', for their healing and helping.

I discovered that these lightworkers also need help themselves. They usually know nothing about starting a business, gaining new customers, and maintaining profitability. They usually settle on very small fees for their work because they feel they are delivering their 'gift', without considering that they have to take care of themselves before they can care for others.

So, I started a business called Lightworker Coach, where I help these people. I currently have around a dozen clients in different parts of the world, and that client list is growing.

My thought process goes something like this: I want to help people raise their frequency and 'move toward the light'. There are already many thousands of lightworkers who are currently helping people in this way. Therefore, when I help the lightworkers, I am helping all of their clients as well – thereby helping a greater number than those I see.

The website for this business is www.lightworkercoach.co.uk and it contains guidance on starting a new business, finding new customers, marketing ideas and tactics on scaling a business to make sure it fulfils the needs of the business owner, as well as their clients.

This information will benefit anyone who is looking to start a new business or to grow the business they already have.

If you have any questions you would like to ask me in this regard then please drop me a line on peter@lightworkercoach.co.uk.

Understanding spirituality

In my opinion, spirituality is not about religious dogma or belonging to a particular faith. Rather, it is the journey of self-discovery, finding meaning, and developing a heightened sense of awareness and connection to something greater than us.

Some view spirituality as an inward search, a way to find their life's purpose and live with authenticity. For others, it involves a profound respect and reverence for nature, art, or the vast mysteries of the cosmos. No matter how you define it, spirituality ultimately guides you to live a more conscious, present, and fulfilling life.

Spirituality is often misunderstood or oversimplified as just a religious practice or belief system. However, it encompasses a much deeper and more profound experience of life itself. Let's take a closer look at what spirituality truly represents:

What is life all about? Spirituality can be a quest to find life's deeper meaning and significance beyond the physical and material world. Spirituality asks the big questions - Why are we here? What is the nature of reality and consciousness? Is there more to existence than what we can perceive with our five senses? On this quest, we begin to realise that we are not merely physical beings having a temporary human experience but are instead eternal spiritual beings temporarily residing in a physical form.

What is our place in life? Spirituality can involve cultivating virtues like compassion, gratitude, humility, and self-awareness. Spiritual growth is profoundly transformative - it reshapes us at the core of our being. As our consciousness expands, we naturally become more compassionate, feeling the inherent interconnection between all life. We experience deeper gratitude for the miracles and beauty surrounding us. And above all, we turn inward to cultivate uncompromising self-awareness and self-inquiry.

Helping you live your own life. Spirituality can help you live with authenticity, aligning your thoughts, words and actions with your core values. When you mature spiritually, you inevitably shed layers and patterns of behaviour, thought and speech that are out of harmony with your deepest truths. You stop living according to others' expectations or society's conditions of "success." Instead, you realign completely with your soul's callings and personal values.

Finding inner peace. Spirituality can enable you to find inner peace in life's chaos and difficulties. The human journey is one of continuous change and inevitable challenges. Spirituality acts as your anchor, allowing you to access a place of inner peace that transcends external circumstances.

Connectedness. Spirituality can encourage harmony with nature, other living beings, and the universe itself – as my awakening did with me. As your spiritual awareness blossoms, the artificial separations between yourself and the world around you dissolve. You experience the cosmos as a vivid, dynamically interconnected web of beings and energies - including the plants, animals, forests, oceans and stars. Rather than feeling isolated, you see yourself as an equal strand in this magnificent fabric.

Ultimately, genuine spirituality is an embrace of life's biggest truths. It is a path toward wisdom, service and realising our highest human potential. While spirituality takes each person on their own unique inward journey, what we gain are virtues that benefit all of humanity and our planet.

As you have already seen with my own take on spirituality, it is not confined to any single religion or belief system. It is a universal human experience that transcends cultures and creeds. We can be spiritual while following a specific faith or embracing secular philosophies. The quest for spiritual growth is deeply personal and unique to each individual.

Practices for spiritual growth

There are many paths to nurture your spirituality. Here are some practices that can enrich your spiritual journey:

Meditation: The ancient practice of meditation allows you to silence the endless mental chatter and restore presence and stillness. As you focus your attention inward on the breath or a mantra, the turbulence of thoughts gradually subsides. In this state of serene presence, you can perceive the true spaciousness of your being beyond the conditioned mind and ego. Meditation cultivates mindfulness, reduces stress, quiets the pull of the outer world, and can offer profound insights into the nature of consciousness itself. Find a meditation practice that resonates and make it a daily ritual. We will speak more about meditation because it is something I use every day since that session in The Bahamas.

Contemplation and reflection: Set aside periods of quiet solitude to contemplatively ponder life's bigger questions and mysteries. What is your soul's purpose? What is the nature of reality, consciousness, and the vast cosmos? What are the core virtues and principles you wish to uphold? Use journaling, silent sitting, or mindful walking to reflect deeply on your values, beliefs, existential wonderings, and what brings you a profound sense of meaning. Explore writings or teachings from spiritual traditions that resonate.

Spending time in nature: Few things inspire awe for the grandeur of creation like immersing yourself in natural landscapes. Go for mindful walks, work in the garden, camp under the stars, or simply sit quietly and observe life unfolding around you. Open your senses to the scents, sounds, textures, and humbling beauty. I have all the wet-weather hiking gear now that I am 'more mature' and get outside for a walk as often as I can – usually up mountains.

Study philosophies and teachings: There are lots of traditions that offer timeless guidance on spiritual living. Explore teachings and philosophies that resonate, like the Yoga Sutras, Tao Te Ching, Buddhist Dharma, the wisdom of indigenous elders, or even secular philosophies. Reading and contemplating sacred texts can inspire shifts in awareness, unlock deep realisations, and bring about personal transformation.

In my case, reading the Bible at a young age did not immediately transform me but now that I'm more mature, things come back to me and have much more resonance now. Another route would be to read works like 'Letting Go' by David R. Hawkins for raising your consciousness. Take a look at "The Nature of Personal Reality" by Jane Roberts for an in-depth study on the workings of the universe. And I feel I must just add 'The Hermetica' by Timothy

Freke and Peter Gandy, which covers everything we have lost over five thousand years regarding our human spirituality.

Creative expression: When we immerse ourselves in creative practices like art, music, dance, or writing, we tune into a mystical channel from Source itself. The creative spark within flows through us, allowing us to birth new worlds, ideas, and expressions into form. Creative expression is a profound spiritual practice. It awakens the senses, allows the soul to speak, and enhances our appreciation for beauty. For me, this means playing guitar. I've never achieved greatness at it and probably never will. But it takes me off into a zone where I'm lost to the world. I don't play in public. I play to 'lose myself' in the moment of creation.

Service and compassion: There is profound spiritual truth in the notion that we are all interconnected, as I now know by experience. By cultivating compassion and extending kindness through service to others, we realise our ultimate nature that transcends the separate self. Volunteer, practice daily acts of generosity and care, and use your unique gifts in service of the greater good. This gets you outside of the enclosed space of your ego and connects you to the vast ocean of humanity itself. True service comes from the heart, not a sense of obligation.

Mindful living: To live mindfully is to embrace each moment with profound presence and intention - not trapped in regrets of the past or fantasies about the future. Savour life's simple pleasures like good company, nourishing foods, and daily activities with great attentiveness instead of mindless habits and distractions. Practice gratitude rituals and live according to your spiritual values and truths, rather than being swept away by cultural currents. Mindfulness keeps you anchored in the unwavering presence of the now.

In addition to mindfulness, I would like to share this quote from Neville Goddard:

"Be conscious of being that which you want to appear."

Because that quote means a great deal to me. It speaks to me of living in the present moment and being deliberate about making yourself into what you would like to become.

There is no singular "right" way to be spiritual. Experiment with different practices and find what resonates most profoundly with your soul. You may be drawn to one path or a combination of several. The key is to approach your spiritual journey with curiosity, openness, and authenticity.

Living with purpose and presence

As your spiritual awareness blossoms, you'll find yourself naturally aligning with a life guided by profound purpose and anchored in present moment awareness. Living purposefully to me means:

Finding your natural ability: Uncover your unique gifts and express them in service of others. Each of us is imbued with innate talents, strengths and creative sparks that are meant to be offered up for the greater good. As you deepen your spiritual journey, you'll experience a calling to uncover and cultivate these gifts. Perhaps you have a natural ability to listen with empathy, a flair for inspiring others through words, or a deep reverence for nature that could nurture environmental stewardship. Our unique talents might allow us to serve people, animals, the environment – or whatever drives you.

Your core values: As spiritual conscious beings, we are ultimately defined by our values and principles, not our egotistical accomplishments or external identities. When you live with purpose, you methodically align each choice, from the mainstream to the mundane, with your most deeply held values like integrity, kindness, simplicity, compassion or global consciousness.

Your contribution: Each of us has a sacred gift to offer humanity during our brief life passage. When you live purposefully, you become committed to blessing the world through your own special contributions and positive impact, no matter how grand or seemingly small. This could mean inspiring the next generation, creating art that awakens others, building a business powered by ethical principles, or simply spreading more kindness in your daily encounters.

When you embrace this purposeful existence, something miraculous occurs - each day takes on profound richness, significance and fulfilment regardless of your external circumstances. You begin experiencing life not as an endless succession of trivial tasks and checklists, but as a magnificent odyssey with opportunities for growth, joy and spiritual Renaissance. Even life's most mundane moments are revealed as gateways into the sacred when perceived through this purposeful lens.

Equally vital to living purposefully is the practice of presence - being fully engaged and attuned to this ever-unfolding Now. So often we let our minds relentlessly cycle through looping narratives about past regrets or anxieties about future events, neglecting the only point of power we actually possess - this present reality before us. This chronic dissociation makes us numb to the opportunities surrounding us each moment. Spiritual practices anchor your consciousness firmly in the here and now, so you can begin relishing life's precious moments and beauty fully once again. This has been very well covered by Eckhart Tolle, in his book "The Power of Now".

Through purpose and presence, the inevitable challenges of human existence become far more navigable. When your core is rooted in meaning and you face life's ups and downs by embracing the present moment, you are able to respond to difficulties with wisdom and grace instead of panic. Your relationships also become revitalised with authenticity, empathy and aliveness now that you show up fully attentive and real in each encounter. Even your relationship with yourself is elevated as you start shedding inauthentic masks and self-deceptions that previously obstructed self-awareness.

Ultimately, when you live with purpose and presence, you realise at your core that you are not simply a separate, disjointed being having a random series of fleeting human experiences. Instead, you are an eternal consciousness with pure presence. Each moment and encounter, no matter how insignificant, is revealed as a doorway into the unified field of universal awareness.

Living purposefully with presence is both the lofty summit of spiritual awakening and paradoxically the most simple, accessible grace.

When you live with intention and purpose, each day takes on greater richness and significance. You experience more joy, gratitude, and contentment, regardless of external circumstances.

Equally vital is the practice of presence – being fully engaged in the here and now. So often, we dwell on the past or worry about the future, missing out on the profound beauty of the present moment.

Through purpose and presence, you'll find that challenges become more manageable, relationships become deeper, and life itself takes on a new quality.

Death, Dying and the Great Mystery

Inevitably, our spiritual exploration leads us to contemplate the great mysteries – the nature of consciousness, what happens after we die, and whether there is an afterlife. While no one can claim to have all the answers, grappling with these profound questions is part of the spiritual passage.

Different philosophies and belief systems offer various perspectives on death and what might lie beyond. Some view it as the end of our consciousness, while others believe the soul transitions to another realm or is reborn into a new existence. Fundamentally, the respect for this great mystery itself is a hallmark of spiritual maturity.

However, you reconcile with this inevitability, death can be a powerful catalyst for spiritual growth and appreciation for the preciousness of life itself. By being present to our mortality, we are reminded to live each day with love.

Be curious: As you contemplate your own beliefs about the great mystery of what lies beyond this life, it's important to approach the subject of death and dying with openness, wisdom and inquiry rather than resistance or fear. Death is an inescapable part of the journey of being human. By facing it with curiosity and courage, you normalise it and find deeper revelations.

Share your thoughts: Have thoughtful, vulnerable discussions with your loved ones about your values, spiritual beliefs, and wishes surrounding your eventual death. Share how you'd like your life celebrated, your legacy honoured, or your body treated according to your traditions. But also, openly discuss your wonderings about the great mystery itself - do you believe in an afterlife, reincarnation, or that consciousness simply dissolves back into the universe?

Show gratitude: Live each precious day as if it were your very last, with profound reverence, gratitude and presence. Let each morning's sunrise be a miracle. Relish the simple majesty of being alive - the smell of coffee, the birdsong outside your window, the smile of a loved one. When you live with this level of appreciation, you open yourself to the sacredness of every moment.

Be compassionate: Cultivate deep compassion - for yourself and for all others who are facing death or grieving the loss of loved ones. Hold spaces for this most tender of human experiences with gentleness, empathy and patience, not dismissing the waves of sadness, fear or regret.

Have faith: Trust that the great cycle of life continues in wondrous ways beyond this physical plane of existence. Our consciousness arises from and merges back into the infinite source that animates all of creation. While we might not be able to perceive what happens after our body's death with our rational minds, we can have faith in the cosmic intelligence. The Divine Spirit if you will.

Death's great mysteries remain one of humanity's most profound contemplations. Treat it with reverence, allow it into your heart, and appreciate the preciousness of life.

The Soul Plan

My personal take on death was cemented after I read 'Your Soul's Plan' by Robert Schwartz. It answered so many questions for me. The author explains that, before we are born, we meet with our 'soul family' and agree our plan for our forthcoming life. The plan is not set in stone and is not a 'scripted' plot that we are supposed to follow. We have choices at every second of our existence and it's the choices we make that determine whether or not we have adhered to the plan. Our soul family will include the souls of our parents, siblings, offspring and others. Our soul plan will help us become more enlightened souls and provide experiences for us to increase our consciousness. Our souls are eternal.

This leads to the concept of reincarnation. The author suggests that we are here on 'school Earth' each lifetime to allow us to learn from our incarnation. And the type of lessons we have to learn are subjects like love, compassion, kindness and so on. This is well described in Sanskrit writings going back over 3,500 years, where they introduced the word 'karma'.

Taking this further, Robert Schwartz suggests that whatever we are here to learn, what karma we have to 'balance', we must learn it from a position of lack.

This really resonated with me. I started to understand the concept when I thought about my own childhood, where I feel there was a lack of love. There were extenuating circumstances so some grace needs to be given. However, I mostly remember being hit more than I remember being given love. My father worked in British Steel in a horrible occupation and so felt justified in spending housekeeping money in the pubs and clubs.

This concept of being here in this incarnation to learn and having to start by being placed into a family where the desired end purpose was lacking, dawned on me. It all fit and suddenly made sense. I then imagined being at the 'soul family' meeting and saying I would like to experience love in this lifetime. Then my soul family agree they will take me on and help me with this quest. So, the first thing they make sure is that there is little or no love during my incarnation with them.

My enduring emotion was anger. Anger from my parents and siblings (except the two younger ones) and my anger back at them because of the frustration I constantly felt. This put me at a huge disadvantage in 'making my way' through life. I was not shown how to give love and receive love. So, personal relationships were tough.

I left school the first chance I had and, as you know, ended up involved in drug and alcohol abuse and finally found myself in prison (young offender's institute) as a teenager. Not the place for an angry young man because all I did was confront a lot of other young men who were also very angry!

It was hard to have a girlfriend for long. When I finally married, I seemed to spend the whole time in a state of anger. This was anger at the world and anger at myself. But everyone around me bore the brunt – my two children and my wife. For which I now apologise and seek forgiveness.

Now I look back and I realise I have learned the lesson of love. In my 'mature years' I understand a great deal more about love and I am much easier about giving and receiving love. That word was never in my vocabulary and now I can say it and mean it.

As a consequence of Robert Schwartz's book, I can look at the soul plan I entered into and congratulate all my family. I can now thank them for their part in my education. Without my parents and siblings being what they were and treating me the way they did, I would not have turned out as strong and positive as I am now.

Simply for clarification, I want to say that I no longer bear anyone any grudges and everyone is forgiven. My parents had no other model than to emulate their own upbringing. So, I have made my peace with the souls of my father and my mother. Now I have them on ‘my team’ looking after me from beyond the veil.

Another point about reincarnation – it means we do not lose loved ones when they pass. We just meet with them again during the ‘between life’ stage and compare notes about our experiences in this life. Consequently, I can honestly say I am no longer in any fear of death and will be delighted when I am taking my last breath. It will mean my karma is balanced and I am about to hang out with my soul family for a while. My little sister passed when she was fifty-two and I am looking forward to laughing with her again.

We think we are human beings having a spiritual experience, whereas we are spiritual beings having a human experience.

Your spiritual journey

Let your spiritual practices be guided by your “inner voice” and intuition, not expectations from others. Trust your instincts – your gut feel. That is the best guide for all of us. Sit quietly and contemplate some of the things that are spoken about in this book. See if some of the ideas here resonate with something inside you.

Seek out communities and kindred spirits who can support you, and don't be afraid to go your own way when needed. The sage within you knows the way – listen and trust that inner wisdom.

Most importantly in my opinion, embody the virtues and qualities your spiritual values uphold: Compassion. Humility. Love. Kindness. Authenticity. Wisdom. Reverence for all life. When you live these ideals wholeheartedly, you become a beacon of inspiration for others.

May your spiritual way be filled with insights, grace, and the profound realisation that you are so much more vast than you ever imagined – an eternal consciousness having a brief, but utterly profound human experience.

More about meditation

We touched on meditation earlier and this is such a big topic I would just like to try to help you if this concept is new to you. Or perhaps you know what it is and I am simply reminding you and prompting you to take up meditation once more. As you have seen earlier, I struggled with this for some time and yet took to it really well once I had a guided meditation in the presence of others more 'enlightened' than me.

With regular practice, you learn to unhook your awareness from the ego-mind. Slowly, you awaken to the true spacious expanse of your being that extends beyond the voice in your head. In this state of unconditioned presence, you can perceive life with clarity, rather than through your own mental filters.

The roots of meditation stretch back thousands of years through countless traditions, each with their own nuances and approaches. Some practices emphasise focused attention on a single object like the breath or a mantra. Others cultivate an open, awareness where you simply witness the endless flow of sensations, thoughts and emotions arising and passing away without clinging to them. Certain styles integrate physical postures and energetic exercises. And still others weave in philosophical teachings and contemplative inquiries.

One way to define meditation is for us to be doing one thing with the whole of our being. That is, bringing our mental focus to a point, and holding it there for increasing lengths of time. I now can see that the effect of such sustained focus results in a state of deep relaxation. And for me it reduces stress. I also understand now that this contributes to our ability to heal ourselves.

Whichever form of meditation you're drawn to, the fundamentals remain the same - using the breath, sound, visualisation or inquiry as a concrete anchor to domesticate the wandering mind. With repeated practice, your ability to remain rooted in present awareness expands. You carve deeper grooves of inner stillness. Slowly, the controlling tendency of the mind relaxes its grip.

The benefits of regular meditation are multifaceted - it reduces stress, enhances focus and emotional intelligence, regulates the fear/anxiety response, and can even improve physical health and well-being. But perhaps most importantly, meditation awakens you to the truth of your fundamental nature beyond the conceptual mind.

I believe that, in my case, meditation allows me to quieten the voice inside my head. I didn't realise that everyone had a 'voice' inside their head that needed to be calmed down. To paraphrase Eckhart Tolle, he said, 'If you tell me you do not have a voice inside your head, it's that voice that is telling you that.'

For millennia, meditation has been the heart-practice for those on the spiritual path, a supremely transformative tool for self-knowledge and inner peace. When you commit to a daily meditation practice, whether 10 minutes or an hour, you are dedicating yourself to a journey of awakening. You are entering the vastness of your own being and perceiving life with presence.

With discipline and patience, the habit of staying present blossoms and you carry a tranquillity into all other aspects of your daily life. Choose a meditation approach that resonates deeply and make it a non-negotiable ritual, as vital as breathing itself.

One day, I am sure, we will include meditation in every school day and teach our children how to calm down the noise.

My approach to meditation

To get started, simply find a comfortable place to sit, whether that's on a cushion, chair or couch. You can even try it lying down at first if sitting upright is too challenging. Gently close your eyes and bring your attention to your breath. There's no need to control it - simply notice the sensation of the air moving in and out of your body.

Your mind will inevitably wander off into thoughts, daydreams or memories. That's totally normal and natural! The moment you notice your mind wandering, just mentally note "thinking" or "wandering" and gently redirect your attention back to the breath. Don't judge or criticise yourself.

My first attempts were very simple. I would focus on my feet, then legs below the knee, then knees and so on up the body, to the head. My mind would start thinking about something I needed to do and – once I realised I had strayed – I would return to my feet and begin the journey up my body again. It was a long time and many practices before I could get all the way to my head without a thought creeping in! The key is maintaining a gentle, friendly curiosity toward whatever arises instead of frustration.

Once I learned about chakras, I used the seven main energy centres in the body for meditation. The word "chakra" comes from the Sanskrit language and means "wheel" or "cycle". They are perceived as a spinning cone of energy. The chakras have been covered in an earlier chapter but just as a quick reminder, they are located along the spine, all in a straight line, from the base to the crown of the head:

Root chakra: Base of the spine

Sacral chakra: Just below navel

Solar plexus chakra: Between the navel and diaphragm

Heart chakra: Middle of the chest, in line with heart

Throat chakra: Located at the throat

Third eye chakra: Middle of forehead, between the eyebrows

Crown chakra: The top of the head

For me, I can tell when the meditation is starting to have an effect and that is when I can no longer 'feel' my limbs. In that early stage, I feel completely relaxed and safe 'inside myself'. When I continue the practice for longer, all sensation from the body is removed. There are no itches to scratch and no discomfort from sitting or lying. I find I can hear extraneous sounds but I can ignore them. I have meditated in a very busy airport and been able to find inner peace.

I have never repeated that 'golden' moment from the retreat but I am having very many relaxing, regenerative sessions now and I absolutely love them.

Recently I became aware that group meditation has a special effect and I would recommend this for you if you have the chance. The reason that the effect is 'special' is that there will be people in the group who are further along the path than you. That means they will be vibrating at a higher frequency and will 'pull up' the group higher in vibration that any single member of the group could go on their own.

Stick with it and be patient with yourself. Starting a meditation practice is like building any muscle - the more you work it out gently and consistently, the stronger it will become over time. When you do this in the morning, your whole day starts feeling a little calmer. And there's another positive for me. During the day if I find an unwanted emotion rising (anger springs to mind!) I can return to the calmness of my earlier meditation and release the anger.

Practices for spiritual growth

Meditation: We have said a lot already about meditation. There are many different meditation techniques to explore, so find one that resonates with you.

Mindfulness: Mindfulness involves being present in the moment and observing your thoughts and feelings without judgment. It can help you cultivate a sense of peace and inner balance.

Gratitude: Practicing gratitude can shift your focus to the positive aspects of your life. Keep a gratitude journal or simply take a few moments each day to reflect on the things you're thankful for. Also, remember from chapter 2 that we are creating our 'world' every day. So, being positive will mean that you create positivity in your life.

Nature: Spending time in nature can be a powerful way to connect with your spirituality. Go for walks, hikes, or simply sit outside and appreciate the beauty of the natural world.

Yoga: Yoga combines physical postures, breathing exercises, and meditation to promote physical and mental well-being. It can help you find balance and inner peace.

Reading: Explore spiritual books, poetry, or other writings that inspire and uplift you. Reading can provide new perspectives and deepen your understanding of spirituality.

Community: Connect with like-minded individuals who share your spiritual beliefs. Joining a spiritual community can provide support, guidance, and a sense of belonging.

Summary

We looked at what spirituality means and I explained how I believe I am spiritual but not religious. I was raised a Christian but I lost belief in the church in my early teens, during my "off the rails" years! By the end of my twenties, I was travelling and meeting and working with people all over the world from many diverse religions. It showed me that it doesn't matter what religion is practiced, it is the person that makes the difference. There are good people in every religion.

My learning about spirituality came late in life when I started to understand that we are all on our own path of enlightenment – it's just that some people don't realise it yet. I love the lyric in "Never Tear us Apart" by INXS, which goes – "I told you, that we could fly, 'cause we all have wings, but some of us don't know why".

My interest in spirituality was cemented after I experienced what spiritual people call an 'awakening'. It was a huge shock to me and the world seemed to change for me, in a positive way.

Spirituality goes beyond the confines of religion. It's a personal journey of connecting with something greater than ourselves, finding meaning in life and cultivating a sense of inner peace. It's about us exploring the depths of our being, discovering our life's purpose and aligning our actions with our beliefs.

Spirituality can involve a connection to a higher power, nature, or our own inner self. It can be a source of comfort, strength, and inspiration. Whether we practice a formal religion or find spirituality in other ways, it's a deeply personal and unique experience.

We have examined death and dying. My outlook on this changed after reading "Your Soul's Plan" by Robert Schwartz and I recommend that book. Reincarnation is a major tenet in most Asian religions. Robert Schwartz looks at it from another angle that, for me, places it outside of religion.

My parting message

It is very important that you understand that you are creating the world in which you live. What you think about, you bring about.

From today, try to show gratitude every day for what you have. Remember to smile because people will ‘mirror’ you – and you create feel-good chemicals, which then increase your mood.

Whatever age you have reached right now can be the most exciting age of your life. Look after yourself physically and mentally to ensure that your twilight years are the most rewarding.

Being old or being retired does not mean you need to live in poverty – quite the opposite. There are lots of things you can do to improve your lot.

You also do not need to live a lonely existence. There are many opportunities to meet new people, doing volunteer work springs readily to mind. And, if you wish it to be so, you can find new love.

I hope you have picked up my enthusiasm for life now that I’m over 70. There are still so many things for us all to do.

We are all on a journey toward the light. My wish for you is that you can make the final part of this journey full of abundance, love and happiness. To help you in that, all I need to do is remind you what you already know intuitively. That is, believe in yourself.

The blessings that I have, I send to you.

Sources of inspiration for this book

Letting Go by David R. Hawkins

The Go-Giver by Bob Burg and John David Mann

You can Heal Your Life by Louise Hay

You Are The Placebo by Joe Dispenza

Your Soul's Plan by Robert Schwartz

Perfect Health by Deepak Chopra

The Hermetica by Timothy Freke and Peter Gandy

The Power of Now by Eckhart Tolle

The Nature of Personal Reality as channelled by Jane Roberts

Simple Wealth, Inevitable Wealth by Nick Murray

The 4-Hour Work Week by Tim Ferris

How to ask me a question

On your business:

www.lightworkercoach.co.uk – peter@lightworkercoach.co.uk

On the topics covered in this book:

peter@padickinson.co.uk

www.ingramcontent.com/pod-product-compliance
Ingram Content Group UK Ltd.
Pitfield, Milton Keynes, MK11 3LW, UK
UKHW050058091025
8304UKWH00011B/165

9 781068 465802